S.T.E.P.S.
FOR
SUCCESS

S.T.E.P.S. FOR SUCCESS

Self-Training in Essential Personal Skills

GORDON WAINWRIGHT

MERCURY

First published in 1992
by Mercury Books
Gold Arrow Publications Limited,
862 Garratt Lane, London SW17 0NB

Set in Sabon by TecSet Ltd, Wallington, Surrey
Printed and bound in Great Britain by
Mackays of Chatham plc, Chatham, Kent

British Library Cataloguing in Publication Data is available

ISBN 1–85251 126–5

CONTENTS

1

INTRODUCTION

We all spend at least ten years of our early lives at school and yet most of us are not very good at using twelve of the essential skills we need to make our way in life.

We leave school – many of us even leave university – without receiving any direct tuition in the following skills:

- How to think clearly and logically (the technical term is *convergent* thinking);

- How to think creatively (the technical term is *divergent* thinking);

- How to remember (using the long-established techniques of mnemonics, some of which go back to at least 500 BC);

- How to study (this one really is surprising – yet most people go through the whole of their education without ever being shown effective ways of learning);

- How to read efficiently (we are taught how to read in primary school and then reading disappears from the curriculum – we do a lot of reading in school, but no one actually shows us how to do it more efficiently);

- How to listen (it is not only a well-known high street bank that has recently appreciated the importance of being able to listen well – some industrial companies are now teaching their employees how to listen efficiently);

- How to write effectively (we seem to spend a great deal of time at school writing – yet no one shows us how to write simply, clearly and concisely, in the way we need to write once we have to start earning a crust);

- How to speak effectively in public (not on grand occasions, but for family affairs like weddings, for business presentations to clients and for communications with employees);

- How to use body language (the non-verbal side of communication is almost totally neglected in our schools and yet here again there are skills that can be improved with the right kind of training);

- How to take part in meetings effectively and how to run them ourselves (no wonder most people who spend a large part of their working hours in meetings think they are a waste of time);

- How to manage people (whether it is those who work for us, those we work for or even the people we live with);

- How to manage our time (effective time management techniques alone could give many people greater control over their lives and more time for the things that really matter, which is why the approach in this book concentrates on techniques of time creation).

All these skills – and I have no doubt we could find many more – yet no one teaches us how to use them more efficiently and effectively. Until now.

This book is about to help you to put matters right.

Here you will learn how to develop your skills in each of these areas and also acquire the techniques for bringing about improvement in any skill which you wish to use more efficiently.

2

S.T.E.P.S.

So what is S.T.E.P.S.?

Quite simply, the letters stand for Self-Training in Essential Personal Skills.

We shall apply the S.T.E.P.S. technique here to each of the twelve skills identified in Chapter 1 as underdeveloped. These skills are essential to our successful performance of any job and, indeed, to leading a useful and fulfilling life generally. In Chapter 15, you will be shown how to apply the technique to improve any other skills which you wish to develop.

Who needs S.T.E.P.S.? Anybody who has not already been trained or who trained themselves in such a way that their skills are already as developed as they are ever likely to be. Moreover, the technique can be applied at any age and by anyone of average or above average intellectual ability. There is no magic about the technique and there is nothing very complicated in applying it. It is based on a combination of common sense and what research has proved are the best ways to proceed in various activities. It does not require any special equipment, other than items which are likely to be available in any modern home.

How does S.T.E.P.S. work? That, clearly, is what this book will explain. But it will help enormously if you bring four basic attitudes or approaches with you as you embark upon the programme.

- You will fare better if you want S.T.E.P.S. to succeed. In other words, it will help if you are motivated. You may still improve even if you are not, but it will help if you are.
- You need to feel confident that, in each of the identified skill areas, improvement is possible. One factor that might help to give you that confidence is to remind yourself that you have not

received this training before and therefore there is a gap between what you have done and what you could have done. This might lead you, quite reasonably, to conclude that some improvement at least ought to be possible. In fact, you might even say it is inevitable.

- Thirdly, you need to try to improve. Some effort will be required. But not too much. You do not want to reach a situation in which the harder you try, the worse you get.
- Last, you will need to persist. You will have to keep taking the tablets!

Once started, you can only expect the programme to succeed fully if you do everything that is asked of you in this book. That means that you will need to set aside time for practice. Once you know how to perform any skill more effectively and efficiently, achieving a higher standard of performance is then largely down to practice. Practice, practice, practice.

Why should you bother? Well, take a look through what is on offer here. Skim through the book. Would it not be beneficial to you to be able to manage your time better? Or to read faster? Or to remember things more easily? Take a look. There are bound to be some areas in which you feel you need, or would like, to improve. You will not be asked to try anything that will cause permanent brain damage. And you can always go back to your old ways of doing things if you really want to.

Before we actually start on the first skill, convergent thinking, there are one or two preliminary matters you need to know. For each skill, you will be taken through a set pattern of activity. First of all, the topic will be briefly introduced. Then your current performance will be reviewed. As you will see, this is easier for some skills than for others, but you will still need to know where your starting point lies. Common problems in using the skill are then outlined. Next, some objectives are set for you to try to achieve. As the book will remind you, you should always identify further, more specific objectives of your own and add these to the list.

The bulk of each chapter is concerned with exploring the various methods of bringing about improvement. Remember, there is no magic formula. You will usually be offered a choice of ways of improving and it will be up to you to select the ones that work best for you and to build upon those. Remember that there is no single solution to any of the problems of skills development. You are not about to be initiated into a secret society. Towards the end of each chapter, you will again review your performance, so that you can see how much you have gained. Methods of continuing to improve will be outlined. A completion checklist follows so that you can assess what you have learned from the chapter. Finally, a Conclusion rounds the chapter off.

You will normally need no more than pen or pencil and writing paper and, of course, a copy of this book. Anything else that is needed will be clearly specified. You should select a place to work where you know from experience that you are unlikely to be interrupted. It should also be somewhere where you know you can achieve your best concentration. Some people can work anywhere and shut out the rest of the world. Many people, however, require conditions of relative quiet if they are to achieve the kind of sustained concentration required for effective learning. You should also select a time of day when you know that you can concentrate best. Most people will find that this is early morning. Some will find the evening better. If you select the evening, avoid working on a skill last thing at night. The reason for this is that the first revision of a topic must take place the *same day*. This will be difficult if you are working right up until bedtime. You will need a notebook in which to keep a record of your progress. This will provide you with essential feedback on your performance and will make progress faster and easier.

Remember that the last thing you will do each night is to review whatever it is that you have learned during the day. So, for the next few weeks at least, you will have to put on one side that tempting novel at bedtime. It is important that you drift off into dreamland mulling over the details of the current topic in your mind.

Now you can move on to Chapter 3 and begin.

3

CONVERGENT THINKING

You can define thinking in many ways. One way is to see it as comprising various approaches to solving problems or to selecting the best courses of action to follow. The two forms that thinking takes under this definition are:

1. Convergent, logical, analytical, often predictable thinking;
2. Divergent, creative, insightful, mainly unpredictable thinking.

We shall learn about divergent thinking in the next chapter. Here we examine convergent thinking and identify some of the ways in which we can improve our use of this essential skill.

Convergent thinking follows the rules of logic and tends to look for a single correct answer. As we study a problem, for instance, we converge, as it were, upon the answer. This kind of thinking is usually used where we can quantify things. We can, therefore, often foretell the results of convergent thinking, once we can see where our thinking leads us.

It is most useful when we have information which can be handled logically. An example might be finding the cause of a mechanical breakdown. If your refrigerator stops working, you check all the possible causes systematically until you identify the fault. Thus, convergent thinking is most effective when there is likely to be a single right answer. It is also effective in analysing both evidence and arguments.

Review

First let us examine our present use of convergent thinking. Study the following information and then write down your solution to the problem before reading on.

> A group of schoolchildren are suddenly taken ill. They have all eaten beefburgers as a part of their school lunch. Children who did not eat the beefburgers or who went home for lunch were not affected. What caused the illness?

Do not read on until you have finished writing your answer.

Superficially, it appears that beefburgers caused the food poisoning. But did food poisoning affect *all* the children who ate beefburgers? Could dirty plates or knives and forks have caused the poisoning? Could one of the staff in the kitchen who handled the beefburgers have passed on another infection? Could he or she have contaminated the beefburgers by handling some toxic substance previously and forgetting to wash his or her hands?

We need to answer a number of questions and explore the problem systematically before we reach a conclusion. You might like to rate your response on the following scale:

+3 You said you were unable to draw a conclusion without answers to the questions asked above;

+2 You said you were unable to draw a conclusion without an answer to one of questions asked above;

+1 You simply said you were unable to draw a conclusion because you needed more information;

0 You did not reach a decision and gave no reason;

−1 You thought the beefburgers probably caused the illness;

−2 You thought the beefburgers almost definitely caused the illness;

−3 You thought there was no question the beefburgers caused the illness.

Problems

How well we think depends largely on how clearly we think. If our thinking is faulty, then what we say or write will be faulty. There are logical processes which thinking should follow if it is to show the proper connections between ideas or between different pieces of information. It must also follow these processes if it is to show the true relationship between one idea, fact, object or event and another. Where we do not follow these processes then any conclusions which we arrive at are unreliable. Any actions we take based on such conclusions may be misguided and possibly even dangerous either to ourselves or to others. An example might be if someone says, 'The company hasn't won a new contract since he became sales manager. It must be all his fault.' It is, however, improbable that a company's fortunes are solely the responsibility of one person. More information is needed before we can reach a conclusion. Or again, if someone says, 'The video recorder was found to be stolen just after he left the house, therefore he must have been the thief.' Many novels, plays and films show that such conclusions can easily be wrong.

If we base our conclusions about ideas, objects, people, events and so on, not on logical thought, but on our emotional reactions to them, we are on dangerous ground. It is not enough that we like or dislike, feel disgust or fear, or experience pleasure or anger; we have to have evidence and reasons. Emotional thinking leads to prejudging, and prejudice is no basis for action in a rational, civilised society. If someone says, 'Actors, with their strange clothes and often strange behaviour, are no better than the other layabouts and spongers that society has to contend with', they are thinking emotionally. The terms used to describe the groups actors are compared with are highly charged with emotional overtones, therefore this will almost certainly render the opinion unsupportable.

It is also true that similarities in appearance between actors and others do not necessarily imply similarities in attitudes and behaviour. Take a statement like, 'In modern society any individuality is immediately stifled or suppressed by the blind demands for conformity from a monolithic bureaucracy.' 'Stifled', 'suppressed', 'blind' and 'monolithic' are all terms designed to provoke strong emotional responses in the minds of readers or listeners.

Thinking can be worse than emotional. It can be dishonest. That is not to say the person who is guilty of it would steal your wallet or handbag, although they may, but that they are not being honest with themselves, and therefore with other people, in their thinking. They shut their minds to the truth, either consciously or through lack of self-insight. Dishonest thinking is common amongst politicians, especially just before an election, or just after one in which they fared badly and wish to place the blame anywhere but on themselves or their own party. Often it also results from special pleading, that is to say from people trying to justify a position apparently rationally, but whose sole objective is that the outcome they argue for will benefit them.

Sometimes thinking lacks clarity simply because it is superficial. Errors and false conclusions occur if an individual does not devote enough time to thinking about a problem or question. It is, however, the kind of thinking that we tend to encourage in an age of mass communication with its demands for instant judgments. You can find evidence of it any day of the week in any newspaper or on any television channel.

Objectives

Before we begin to consider the methods by which we can improve convergent thinking, we need to bear in mind the objectives we are seeking to achieve. You should add some specific objectives of your own to the list. These are simply the basic objectives you should have:

- Recognising problems, tasks and other situations which require a convergent thinking approach;
- Maintaining objectivity in thinking;
- Using methodical approaches in thinking;
- Distinguishing clearly between fact and opinion.

Methods

If we are to avoid the problems in thinking discussed above, our thinking should possess certain qualities.

We should be aware of logical processes. Working through this chapter should help to make you more aware of these. Basically, logical thought concerns itself with the relationships between statements rather than with the truth or falsity of the statements. It is possible to arrive at a logical conclusion which is untrue, if the original statements were untrue. However, the test to prevent this happening lies in basing statements on evidence. A logical conclusion, then, is one which follows inescapably from what has been stated previously, for instance:

'Students are all troublemakers.'
'Philip is a student.'
'Therefore, Philip is a troublemaker.'

We know that this conclusion may not be true, but it follows logically from the previous statements. An awareness of logic helps us to recognise whether fallacies in our thinking arise from faulty information or faulty thought processes. It is only when we know the source of any error that we can begin to do something to remedy it. The above example highlights the fact that logical thinking on its own does not necessarily lead to clear thinking.

We should avoid emotional reactions. We can never exclude altogether the presence of emotion in our reactions to statements, situations, issues or problems, but, if we are aware of when we react emotionally, we can begin to lessen the influence this has over our thinking. If we want to think clearly, this self-awareness and self-insight is essential, for it is difficult, if not impossible, for the emotional and prejudiced person to think rationally and reasonably. Useful discussion should, therefore, be a cool, dispassionate process.

We should be honest in our thinking. We need to be especially honest about our own motives. We may choose to hide those motives from others to achieve a specific objective, but we should never delude ourselves about what it is we really want. This self-examination is another essential part of the process of thinking clearly. It also helps, of course, if we are honest with one another, even over motives. This way we are much more likely to arrive at the truth.

We should give adequate consideration to the matters about which we think. This does not refer simply to the need to allow sufficient time for consideration, but also to the need to have enough evidence on which to base a conclusion. In other words, before we can decide whether the stated relationships between facts (and hence the conclusions drawn from them) are correct, we must first check the accuracy of the facts.

Thus, we can identify three stages in the process of allowing adequate consideration:

- Check the accuracy of the information available as thoroughly as possible within the time available;
- Check the validity of the relationships claimed to exist between various pieces of information;
- Check the logical validity and the truth of the conclusions drawn by referring back to the information from which they stem.

Given this kind of approach as a basis, there are also some common fallacies in thinking which we should try to avoid. There are twelve that we shall consider here. These are the ones that we can most readily and most frequently identify in newspapers and on radio and TV.

The first is over-generalising. It is essential that we can, from the mass of particular and specific information which confronts us, identify and use certain generalisations. We have to have general rules and principles for guidance, which we can modify, if necessary, in particular circumstances. We simply do not have the time to assess everything on its individual merits on each occasion.

Of course, if something is important enough then we must find the time, but in everyday life we cannot always achieve the ideal situation. However, dangers arise if we over-generalise or over-simplify to the extent that we condemn a whole class of people or things for a characteristic or fault possessed by some, or even many, of them (for example, 'Students are all troublemakers'). It is also dangerous to link two statements together when they are not necessarily logically connected (for example, 'Allowing high inflation is wrong because it is the people on fixed incomes who suffer'. The inflation might not necessarily affect the items that people on fixed incomes are restricted to buying). We should avoid jumping to conclusions. Because careful thinking takes time and because we tend to rely too much on what we have learned from previous experiences, we can arrive at conclusions too quickly. Often this process is so rapid and the time for reflection so short that we can be said, quite justifiably, to jump straight from an initial awareness to a conclusion.

As you might expect in such circumstances, many conclusions arrived at in this way are erroneous and provide an inadequate basis for decision making or action on our part. We read in a newspaper: 'A man is helping the police with their inquiries.' We jump to the conclusion that the police have detained the person who is guilty of the crime they are investigating. True, the statement is often used as code for precisely this, but there are many occasions on which it is not.

We also tend to jump to conclusions about people's motives for doing things. A politician speaks out in favour of more help for homeless people. We conclude immediately that she is doing this merely to score a party political point off her opponents or because there are more homeless people in her constituency than in others. When we jump to a conclusion in this way, we may be right but we are quite often likely to be wrong.

We should not get too personal. We are prone to believe that sensible arguments cannot possibly come from unwise people. It is not necessarily true that if we can ridicule a person then we can also ridicule his or her arguments. Many apparently irrational and eccentric people can present a logical defence or repudiation of a position. We should take care to focus our attention on the argument itself rather than on the personality behind it. Similarly, we should, if we wish to argue honestly, avoid personal attacks on our opponents in the hope that this will either discredit their arguments or that they will become angry and thus argue less effectively. Such attacks may help to win political or debating points, but they do nothing to encourage clear thinking and reasoned discussion.

'The pan calls the kettle black' is a metaphorically expressed form of the line of reasoning that runs, 'My argument is a poor one but so is yours, so that makes us even.' This is by no means necessarily true for it is not always a case of being wholly right or wholly wrong. There are degrees of rightness and wrongness and we do not necessarily have to remedy all the faults in an argument before we can prefer it to another. Often we must base a decision on the least of several evils rather than on the best of all the available possibilities. We must also consider the relative relevance of arguments to the point at issue before we can decide which faults in them are significant and which are not.

Faulty reasoning over cause and effect usually takes the form: 'Event B followed event A, therefore event A caused event B.' Succession is no evidence of causation and we need to identify a much closer link than that of mere timing before we can conclude justifiably that a preceding event caused a subsequent one. This logical fallacy may account for the origin of many of our superstitions and old wives' tales.

False analogy arises from comparing two apparently similar events or situations and saying, 'This event is like that one, therefore the outcome will be the same.' Unless the world has suddenly become completely predictable, we have little justification for a such a conclusion. We must always make comparisons with great caution. We must not only ensure that two events or situations are alike in certain respects but that they are alike in the respects that matter to our argument. Even then there is no guarantee of similarity of outcome or anything else. Arguing by analogy is very entertaining and can help to make a situation dramatically clear, but can be misleading unless we are extremely careful in applying the technique.

We tend to pay much more attention to an argument if it is put forward by someone who is an acknowledged expert in a particular field or even if he or she is simply well qualified or well known. This is perhaps inevitable and, in certain circumstances, quite justifiable, but we should always remind ourselves of the dangers in doing this. In scientific and technical matters, for example, we often have to accept the word of the expert because we are not sufficiently knowledgeable to be able to challenge it. We should still be on our guard against accepting illogical conclusions from such people and we should be suspicious of so-called experts in many areas of political, social and economic affairs. Quite often the experts are no better able to arrive at valid conclusions than non-experts. We should use experts to obtain as many facts as possible, but we should then draw our own conclusions.

If we use figures to support an argument, we should always examine them carefully for they may be misleading. We should always check, as far as possible, their accuracy. We should also subject them to a test of relevance, for, whilst they may impress us, they may not directly affect the particular argument in hand. It is also worth bearing in mind that introducing too much statistical information into an argument will often confuse rather than clarify. We need to take particular care with propositions like one quarter, one third or a half for they are very approximate and can be abused. 'Nearly a half' sounds more convincing than '40 per cent' or 'over a third' and we may distort an argument by such free use of figures. Similarly, in stating, say, that 55 per cent of people are in favour of a particular course of action, we should remember that they may support it only half-heartedly and from an ill-informed point of view, whereas 45 per cent of well-informed people may strongly oppose it.

Very few people indeed can claim total lack of prejudice and that number is highly unlikely to include anyone using this book – or even its author. It is therefore easy to win over an opponent if you can identify and exploit his or her prejudices. Likewise, it is also easy for your opponents to win you over. There is no place for prejudice in reasoned argument and, whilst we may never eliminate it altogether, we should continually try to raise the level of debate above mere slogan swapping. Some common prejudices to which we can make appeals are:

- Foreigners are untrustworthy and unreliable;
- People from certain countries are inferior in intelligence;
- Young people are more immoral in their behaviour than older people;
- Trade unionists only want to obtain more money for less work;
- Employers only want to get as much work out of people as possible for the lowest possible wage;
- Women are far worse drivers than men;
- A woman's place is in the kitchen;
- Beer brewed in the North is stronger than that brewed in the South.

Most of these and similar prejudices can be refuted by reliable evidence, but many people still refuse to abandon them. Prejudice is, in fact, one of the most difficult obstacles that reasoned argument has to try to overcome.

Self-evident truths, as they are called, are usually prefaced with phrases such as, 'Everybody knows that . . .', when often the reverse is true. It is safer to assume that no truth is self-evident and that we should support every statement by at least some objective evidence. There are very few facts and opinions that are so universally acceptable that no argument about them is either possible or necessary. Even for the few that we can generally accept (for example, that cannibalism is not a permissible activity in a civilised society) the clear thinker should have sound arguments to support them.

We tend to reduce arguments to two opposing sides. We like to see issues in terms of right or wrong, black or white, one thing or another. This process is called polarisation and we expect those who occupy central positions to support one side or the other. We tell them to 'come down off the fence'. This liking for bi-valued judgments causes many errors in thinking, especially where there are valid viewpoints coming between the two extremes. If we are to encourage clear thinking, we should allow multi-valued judgments and see the shades of grey between the polarities of black and white. If we did, we might come a good deal closer to the truth on many more matters than we do at present. Few things in life are simple enough to allow a clear 'Yes' or 'No' answer or to permit outright and unqualified acceptance or rejection.

We judge people partly by the company they keep, but to base the whole judgment on this one aspect is to wander into areas of unsound reasoning. It is simply not good enough to say, 'He mixes with criminals, therefore he is a criminal himself.' He may, of course, be a plain-clothes detective. We have to take great care when forming conclusions about people, events, situations or problems based on the people or objects associated with them. It is never enough to base conclusions merely on associations: we must find other evidence. Otherwise there is too much danger that we shall make mistakes.

If we can, in our own thinking, guard against the twelve fallacies in thinking considered in this section, we shall become progressively more able to detect fallacies in the thinking of others. We shall draw fewer false conclusions ourselves and we shall be adversely affected less often by the false conclusions drawn by others. Knowledge of the sources of errors in thinking should lead us to greater skill in recognising errors whenever and wherever they occur. Recognition should lead us to their avoidance or correction. Thus we begin a process in which our ability to think clearly and convergently improves continuously.

We should remember that, in addition to occurring quite unconsciously, each of the above fallacious ways of thinking can be used deliberately to confuse, mislead and probably defeat an opponent. Watch any party political broadcast or, for that matter, any TV commercial if you wish to see this happening.

Evaluation

Identify the fallacies in thinking in each of the following statements:

1 Just as a pendulum swings backwards and forwards, we shall replace this government by one of an opposite persuasion at the next general election;
2 When I carry my rabbit's foot around with me I never have any bad luck;
3 She is bound to be intelligent because she is always reading;
4 Whenever trade unions get pay increases prices go up, so it is trade unions that cause inflation;
5 I may not prove conclusively that I am right, but you cannot prove that I am wrong, so I win the argument by default;
6 Those who are not with us are against us;
7 Professor Gregory McTavish says, in his standard work on the subject, 'Small men are aggressive through a basic sense of inferiority';
8 'The personnel manager is seen too much in the company of one of the shop stewards for us to take him into our confidence,' said the managing director;
9 No one can deny the justice of our cause.

See page 187 for the answers to these questions.

Ongoing

Some activities and questions which will promote the development of skill in thinking clearly and convergently are these:

- Select an issue on which you feel strongly and write a statement of your views. Let your hair down! Put it to one side for twenty-four hours and then read it again. You should find that you can now identify several things that you would tone down or change in some other way to make the piece more objective and logical.
- Decide how you would determine the truth or falsity of the following statements. Which ones can you not check for their validity?

a) The Swedes read more newspapers than any other nation;
b) The Swedes are the best informed people in the world;
c) The Swedes are the most intelligent people in the world;
d) More copies of newspapers per 1000 population are sold in Sweden than in any other country;
e) Newspapers can range in size from a double sheet to a hundred or more pages;
f) Newspaper circulation is no guide to levels of literacy in a country.

- List examples that you can think of where people follow the rules of logic but the conclusions are false.
- List ways in which people might reduce prejudice.
- List factors which prevent people being honest with each other in argument.
- What difficulties might we encounter in checking the factual accuracy of information?
- Study a daily newspaper and see how many of the fallacies in thinking discussed in this chapter you can find.
- Watch a party political broadcast on TV and list the fallacies in thinking that you notice. You will find this exercise easier to do if you can tape the broadcast and analyse it at leisure later.
- Watch a collection of commercials on TV, and see how many fallacies in thinking you can identify. This, too, is easier if you first tape the commercials.
- Select an opinion on an issue with which you violently disagree. Write a defence of it from the point of view of a supporter.

Completion checklist

At the end of this chapter, you should be able to answer the following questions:

1 List three characteristics of convergent thinking.
2 What kind of thinking is worse than emotional thinking?
3 What are the three stages in the process of allowing adequate consideration?
4 How many fallacies in thinking can you name?
5 List four common prejudices to which we can make appeals.
6 What are the words that usually preface self-evident truths?

7 What is the process of reducing arguments to two opposing sides called?

Conclusion

We have now taken our first step in the improvement of our personal skills. As you move to the next chapter, do not forget about this one. You must not take the view, 'Well, I've done Convergent Thinking – what's next?' It is important to keep what you have learned in mind as you go along. Indeed, every now and then, you should look back over the chapters you have already worked through, just to remind yourself of the important points. The whole process of S.T.E.P.S. is like driving a car – you do not forget one skill when you move on to learn another: you cannot afford to; it is hazardous to your health and to that of anyone else on the road at the same time. Here, the consequences would not be quite so drastic, but it remains true that we should have all our skills ready for action at all times.

One other point to remember before moving on. It is best to start a new subject on a new day. That way there is less risk of one chapter being confused with another.

Review what you have learned from this chapter before you go to sleep tonight.

4

DIVERGENT THINKING

Divergent thinking follows few rules. It does not seek a single correct answer, nor indeed necessarily any answer at all. Starting from a problem, a situation, or a body of information, it diverges, explores, seeks, and examines things from as many viewpoints as possible. It is curious, provocative, controversial, and even ridiculous (it was the odd idea of an eccentric that put the Plimsoll line on ships, for example). We use it especially to find new solutions to old problems, new ways of doing things and different approaches to a wide variety of concerns. It is unpredictable both in method and results. It is most effective where logical approaches have failed, where there is insufficient information for us to use them, or their use is inappropriate for any one of a number of reasons.

Divergent thinking is effective when the probability that there is a single right answer is low or when we have to make an unusual, out of the ordinary, insightful interpretation of the facts to find one. It is effective in opening up new fields for exploitation and new areas for development.

Review

How good a divergent thinker are you at the moment? Try this little exercise:

How many ways can you think of for fastening sheets of paper together?

Here are six to start you thinking:

1 Using staples;
2 Using paper clips;
3 Sellotape;
4 Turning the corners over and tearing them;
5 Welding them – if the paper has some plastic content;
6 Using sealing wax.

Allow yourself no more than 10 minutes and see how many ways you can think of.

Do not read on until you have completed the exercise.

Exercise review

Even a fairly uncreative person should have been able to produce about 10–15 ideas in the time without too much trouble. Not all the suggestions will be new, but this does not matter. In the list below, perhaps only items 5 and 18 offer possibilities of a new method.

If we could weld paper as we can weld plastic bags by the simple, brief application of heat or pressure, each sheet of paper would contain its own built-in fastener. A silver or gold plated nut and bolt would provide a more reliable, yet decorative, method of keeping papers together than a paperweight. One would simply have to punch a hole in one corner of each paper and a device for doing this could be included in the design.

So, possible responses to the question are (including the six we started with):

1 Using staples;
2 Using paper clips;
3 Sellotape;
4 Turning the corners over and tearing them;
5 Welding them – if the paper has some plastic content;
6 Using sealing wax;
7 Split-end pins;
8 Putting a length of wire through and twisting the ends together;
9 Putting in a file or folder;
10 Using string, cotton or wool to tie them together;
11 Using butter, treacle or jam – even water;
12 Pasting them together at the corners or down one edge;
13 Chewing gum;

14 Putting a pin through with a belt of gummed tape linking the ends of the pin;
15 Clips of various kinds;
16 Spring binders;
17 Spit;
18 Nut and bolt, made of gold or silver and decorated;
19 Putting a rubber band round them;
20 Using a hairgrip;
21 Using a safety pin.

You will notice that ideas do not have to work to qualify, nor do they have to be sensible. Sometimes the most impracticable and strange ideas can produce exciting, novel and outstandingly successful solutions. We do not judge at this stage. We simply collect. The time for judgment, as we shall see, comes later.

Problems

One of the most difficult problems facing those new to divergent thinking is that of producing a large enough sample of ideas, interpretations or approaches from which to select the most appropriate one to the task in hand. The more ideas you can generate, the better the chance of finding one that will work. Practice in using the techniques described below soon begins to increase the number of ideas produced. Another problem is simply a lack of knowledge of the techniques to use to generate ideas. Once you have read the next section, this should no longer be a problem.

Lack of opportunity is another factor which restricts many people from being more creative. So many jobs simply do not require anything more than a routine approach to tasks that people in them find that no one encourages their ability to think divergently – indeed, may even actively discourage it. Consequently, lack of practice in divergent thinking becomes another problem. If you practise the techniques described here, this should no longer be the case.

There is also a feeling amongst many people that creative thinkers are born and not made. Whilst it may be true that those who achieve the heights of expertise in any area of human activity usually do so on the basis of an exceptional degree of natural talent, it is still a fact that here, as in any other skill, almost anyone can improve performance if they have the necessary knowledge, guidance and opportunity for practice. The first two can be found here in this book. All you have to do is find the motivation and the time to put them into practice.

Objectives

The basic objectives you should have (though you should, of course, add some specific ones of your own to the list) are:

- Recognising divergent thinking opportunities;
- Trying to put divergent thinking techniques into practice;
- Using methods appropriate to the precise nature of the problem, situation or issue in order to generate novel solutions and responses;
- Getting as much practice as possible in using divergent thinking techniques.

Methods

Although divergent thinking is, typically, unpredictable, there are certain basic principles and approaches which will help to stimulate divergent thinking. They are of particular value to those who are more familiar with the approaches of convergent thinking than with being creative.

First of all, you should define the problem, situation or issue. Write it down. This is necessary to give the thinking and discussion a focal point; it will also help to reveal whether or not the subject is one in which divergent thinking can help. For instance, in industry, divergent thinking is of more use in finding a name for a product or in producing marketing ideas for a product than in deciding whether or not to build a new factory in a particular place. The last problem should be capable of solution by logical approaches.

Second, there are at least eight techniques which you can apply to produce creative answers, solutions and suggestions. You should work systematically through the list until you have developed a reasonable amount of self-confidence in thinking divergently. These techniques are as follows:

- **Producing ideas (any ideas):** Find as many ways as possible of doing or looking at something. Reject nothing. However unpromising an idea looks at first, it may acquire significance later.

- **Questioning what happens at present:** Is it really like this? Does it have to be like this? Is there really a problem? Could we look at things in some other way?

  Example:
  The problem of strikes in industry. You might ask questions such as these: Are there really so many strikes? What is a strike? How are the figures compiled? If we had more holidays, would this reduce the number of strikes? If working conditions were a little better, would this reduce strikes? If management treated workers more as equals, would this reduce strikes? How does our strike record compare with that of other countries? Are strikes evenly distributed throughout industry or are a handful of companies responsible for most of the strikes? Should we even encourage some strikes as a means of allowing people to let off steam? Or as a means of cutting costs in industries that are going through a recession and for whose products there is a temporary reduction in demand?

  In seeking answers to questions like these, we might very well encounter some surprising answers which could have a revolutionary effect on our concept of what strikes really are and on our attitudes towards them.

- **Achieving a new perspective:** Turn things completely round or upside down. If, for example, a building contractor is designing a new kind of house, he or she might consider putting the bedrooms downstairs and the living room upstairs. This might in fact be the best way of doing things if the houses are built on the side of a hill. The builder could put the service roads above the backs of houses and then the living rooms would give better views over the surrounding countryside if they were upstairs. The same idea might work in towns, with underground bedrooms for shift workers, who may need peace and quiet in the daytime.

- **Making comparisons:** Compare the problem, situation or issue to another. They need not be related for this technique to work.

For example, comparing roads to railways may trigger the idea of small, uniformly sized units that could be coupled together and so reduce the traffic in towns whilst preserving the individuality and the privacy of the car. Again, comparing cars to beads (an unlikely analogy) could lead to the same kind of solution and might even suggest a method of linking car-like units together.

- **Allowing ridiculous ideas:** The motor car, aeroplane and submarine were once ridiculous ideas (not to mention going into space).

- **Waiting for inspiration:** Doing nothing or allowing a period of mental 'incubation' is a useful creative thinking technique because once we have stated the problem and defined it the brain will continue to work on it and possible solutions may come to mind at the most unexpected times. Solutions discovered in this way are often revolutionary and yet highly practical.

- **Being ready for sudden and unexpected insights:** This involves readiness twenty-four hours a day for the solution to present itself. If it does, we should note it down straightaway. Many good ideas thought of at 1 a.m. have vanished by 8 a.m. This method differs from waiting for inspiration in that we *actively* think about the problem, situation or issue from time to time. When illumination comes, you are ready for it.

- **Repeating the process:** Going over the same ground again often produces an additional idea which turns out to be the one that will work.

The third step in this approach to creative thinking is to take all ideas, interpretations, insights and solutions that have been produced and evaluate them. The process of evaluation is best carried out by a group of people. You should aim to try to identify the idea or solution which is most likely to succeed and which therefore is the one to try first.

Many people cannot think divergently because they are quite content to accept things as they are. Even if they seek change, they look for improvements based on keeping things pretty much as they are. Change, in these circumstances, becomes minimal and to all intents and purposes the problems remain, the situation continues or the issues persist unresolved.

You should acquire the habit of querying everything. Why is it like this? Why do we do it this way? 'Why?' is the most creative question you can ask, because it is the necessary first step to seeking new ideas. Unless you challenge what is, you will never know what could be. You can increase your facility to do this using much the same methods as for collecting quantities of ideas. You pose a question and then, within a time limit, you discuss the question freely and tape or note down all the solutions offered. They are thus available for evaluation later. At least twenty-four hours should elapse before this evaluation takes place – this enables everyone involved to stand back, detach themselves from the question and then return to it with a greater degree of objectivity. A day later it is possible to look at what you have done almost as if someone else had done it. You can, as it were, get a second opinion from yourself.

Although people have used this technique for many years, brainstorming is still controversial. I include it here in the belief that it has a great deal to offer in producing ideas. Brainstorming sessions are usually group affairs, with everyone sitting around and throwing ideas into a common pool for later evaluation. Evidence has proved, however, that more (and better) ideas are produced when people work individually on a topic than when they work as a group. The best procedure to use, then, is as follows:

- The group should select the subject for brainstorming;
- Each member of the group should operate in this exercise as an individual until the evaluation session and should write on his or her own;
- You should devote ten minutes to a warm-up session. Each person should write down as many solutions to a specimen problem as he or she can think of in the time;
- You should then write up on a flipchart the main subject for brainstorming or otherwise display it for all to see;
- The brainstorming session proper should follow and should last for about thirty minutes. The eight techniques described earlier may be used at any time an individual desires;

- Each person should write down as many solutions to the problem as he or she can think of in the time. You should censor no solution at this stage;

- You should collect all solutions at the end of the brainstorming session;

- You should photocopy or otherwise reproduce the solutions so that everyone can have a copy of every solution. There should then be an evaluation session, in which the group, in discussion, seeks to identify the most productive responses.

It is of course, possible for you to brainstorm on your own and if you are working alone you will need to adapt these eight steps accordingly.

Remember, divergent thinking techniques are of most use in finding new things to do, new ways of doing things, new interpretations and new outlooks. They are invaluable not only in promoting change and development, but also in indicating precisely where and in which ways change and development can take place.

Evaluation

Here is a little test to help you to decide how well you have grasped the principles of divergent thinking:

1 The ability to think creatively:
a) is innate
b) can be learned
c) is confined to very few people
d) is a gift

2 One difference between divergent and convergent thinking is that divergent thinking is:
a) analytical
b) predictable
c) logical
d) unpredictable

3 The first step in thinking divergently is to:
- *a) define the objectives of the thinking*
- *b) exclude the possibility of silly answers*
- *c) analyse the situation*
- *d) state and define the topic*

4 Divergent thinking techniques can be applied to:
- *a) all problems*
- *b) most problems*
- *c) some problems*
- *d) certain problems*

5 In thinking divergently you should:
- *a) allow strange ideas*
- *b) discourage strange ideas*
- *c) encourage strange ideas*
- *d) disallow strange ideas*

6 An important method in divergent thinking is:
- *a) to assemble as many ideas as possible*
- *b) to concentrate on creative ideas*
- *c) to select the best ideas as you proceed*
- *d) to reject nine ideas out of ten*

7 A divergent thinker must:
- *a) question nothing*
- *b) ask the right questions*
- *c) question everything*
- *d) ask sensible questions*

8 You can stimulate the ability to think divergently if:
- *a) there is no set task*
- *b) the task is a familiar one*
- *c) there is a set task*
- *d) the task is an unimportant one*

9 Brainstorming is:
- *a) a method of changing people's opinions*
- *b) a dangerous technique to be applied carefully*
- *c) a method of stimulating creative thought*
- *d) a method of restricting creative thought*

10 The divergent thinker, when producing ideas, tends to work better:
   a) alone
   b) in a group
   c) with someone else
   d) with an experienced thinker

See page 187 for the answers to these questions.

Ongoing

Activities which will promote the development of divergent thinking are asking questions like these:

- How many uses can you think of for a drawing pin?
- How many ways can you use clear plastic sticking tape?
- How many ways can you hang a picture on a wall with no picture rail?
- How many ways can costs be cut in business or industry?
- How many uses can you find for scrap metal?
- How many uses for a desk letter tray?
- How many uses for old newspapers?
- What alternatives are there to paying people for working?
- Why are rooms rectangular and box-shaped? What alternatives are there?
- How would you design a better mousetrap?
- How would you design a cheap, effective household burglar alarm that does not use electricity?

Completion checklist

At the end of this chapter you should be able to answer the following questions:

1 When is divergent thinking most effective?
2 What is one of the most difficult problems which faces those new to divergent thinking?
3 What is the first task in the process of thinking divergently?
4 How many of the eight techniques of divergent thinking can you list?
5 What is brainstorming?
6 When are divergent thinking techniques of most use?

Conclusion

We have now taken the second step in improving our personal skills (that is, assuming you are working through this book as it is presented – you may, of course, simply look at those skills in which you have decided you want to seek personal improvement).

We need to keep the techniques of both steps in mind as we move on to the third area; this is the techniques of improving memory, since unless we can retain ideas and facts we shall have very little to think about, be it convergently or divergently.

Review what you have learned from this chapter before you go to sleep tonight.

5

EFFICIENT MEMORY

Surgeons in the United States are said to have discovered that patients undergoing certain kinds of brain operation, during which they have to remain conscious, report experiencing remembered sensations, smells and pictorial images when the surgeon stimulates the brain. It does not necessarily seem to be stimulation in the same place which produces the recall. Nor does any one part of the brain seem to be the repository for any particular kind of memory. It seems that memories reside in many parts of the brain.

If this is true, it may account for the fact that when a name, for example, is on 'the tip of your tongue', it can take some time before it actually 'pops up' into your consciousness. Presumably a lengthy search has had to take place, as it might in a computer looking for a word in its thesaurus, before the name is found.

It may help here to underline the complexity of memory and the difficulty of finding a single universally agreed definition of what it is and how it works. Generally speaking, memory consists of three elements: acquiring whatever it is we want to remember, storing it, and recalling it. As we shall see, it is at the point of recall that we experience most difficulties, but, because memory is partly a series of skills, training can help to improve significantly the chances of recalling things when required. Often the problem is not that we do not remember the information, but that we cannot recall it. In other words, the information is available, in the sense of being somewhere in the brain, but it is not accessible. In this chapter, we shall see what can be done to improve accessibility.

Review

Take these six items which might typically feature in a shopping list, and memorise them. It should only take you a few minutes:

1 Eggs
2 Tomatoes
3 Washing up liquid
4 Large envelopes
5 A box of tissues
6 A tidy bin

Wait 20 minutes before continuing.

Now, see if you can remember them. You may well have forgotten at least one.

Wait 20 minutes before continuing.

At this point, try to memorise them again. As you try to do this, use a little story to help you. You have been shopping and you are carrying eggs in one hand and tomatoes in the other. As you walk home, you slip on some washing up liquid which someone has spilt and all the eggs are broken and all the tomatoes squashed. You clear up the mess by using the tissues and drop the used tissues into the large envelopes and put the whole lot into the tidy bin.

Wait 20 minutes before continuing.

Finally, see if you can still remember the story and hence the list. You should find that you can. If you think that this is because they are the same items that you tried to remember the first time, substitute them with items of your own choosing. The important thing to do is to construct a little story which incorporates each item at some stage or other.

Problems

One problem, as with most of the skills covered in this book, is that there is no single, simple, magic solution to memory problems. Some techniques will work for some people and other techniques will work for others. You will have to explore what is on offer here, experiment and decide what works best for you. Remember also that, just because a technique does not seem to work very well the first time you try, it does not mean it will not work after two or three attempts. Persevere a little before you give up.

We can create problems for ourselves if we are not selective enough or if we try to remember the wrong things. You cannot, after all, remember everything and there is no point in cluttering up your brain with all kinds of useless information that would only be of use to a contestant on a quiz programme. You have to consider *why* you wish to remember something.

We may experience difficulties because we simply do not know enough about how memory works. There is not the space here to embark upon lengthy explanations of this kind. This is intended to be a practical book. If you require more information about what memory is and about the various theories of how it works, you should read one of the books on memory listed in the Further Reading section at the end of this book.

We may have a problem because we forget. There can be several causes for forgetfulness. The material may not be interesting; we may not really need to remember it; we may not have concentrated well enough when we tried to remember it; it may be a long time since we committed the information to memory and we have not required the material before. The impression, if you like, has simply faded through neglect. Probably the most common memory problem is that very few of us are aware of the techniques that we should use to remember things. No one has ever taught us these. Our educational system assumes that training in memory improvement is not the role of schools. Memory experts often say that there is no such thing as a bad memory, there is only an untrained memory. This may be a somewhat extreme view, but there would appear to be more than just a grain of truth in it.

Objectives

The basic objectives you should have (though you should, of course, add some specific objectives of your own to the list) are:

- Having a better understanding of how memory works in practice;
- Deciding what you need to remember;

- Selecting the most appropriate method for memorising different kinds of information;
- Learning a variety of mnemonic (memory aiding) techniques;
- Practising mnemonic techniques regularly.

Methods

Before we examine some techniques of remembering more effectively, it will be useful to bear in mind that information should possess some or all of at least seven characteristics to ensure that the techniques will work better.

1 Information should possess the quality of **meaningfulness**. In other words, things are easier to remember if they are relevant to us. It is, of course, possible to remember things that are irrelevant. Most of us carry around a stock of 'Not many people know that' kind of useless bits of information. But we shall make better use of our memories if we can concentrate on things that have meaning.

2 **Organisation** makes things easier to remember. If we can identify the underlying structure of the information, it is more likely to register with us. Random facts may stick, but they will stick much more firmly if we organise them in a coherent way.

3 **Association** is an important feature of ease of recall. If we can associate what we want to remember with something that we already know, this will help. We can then link these associations to form patterns. The exercise in the Review section above is an example of this process at work. The association between each item was that of the familiar shopping list. The story linked them and the full story was the pattern that held them all together and increased the chance of recall when required. You may perhaps remember the sequence:

Associations – Links – Patterns

by using the mnemonic acronym **ALP**. There is more about acronyms (words formed from the initial letters of the words to be remembered) and their use in memorising later in this section.

4. **Visualisation** helps. If you can picture what you wish to remember in your mind's eye, this strengthens the impression it makes. This is easier for concrete or 'hard' facts, but it is still

possible for abstract concepts. We may remember a word like 'democracy', for instance, by picturing a ballot form inserted into a ballot box or a word like 'justice' with an image of a pair of scales. We often talk of the scales of justice.

5 Sometimes the problem is that we have simply not given the information enough **attention.** We have just not tried to remember it or we have not really concentrated fully at the time. Obviously one cannot expect to remember things if they have not been given proper attention.

6 **Interest** is an important factor in remembering. You have to have a reason for remembering something or there has to be some other kind of motivation for doing so. Motivation is an important element of success in improving any skill and memory is no exception.

7 Finally, it helps to remember things if you can provide yourself with **feedback** on how well it has registered. A simple technique called 'self-recitation' helps here. Put whatever it is you have tried to memorise to one side. Take a blank sheet of paper and see how much of it you can recall. The more fully you are able to recall the information, the more firmly it has registered.

If some or all of these qualities are present in the information or in your approach to it, the task of memorising is made much easier. It is also made easier if we reinforce the information in some way. That is to say, we take certain steps to ensure that the impression is made stronger. There are several ways of doing this:

- *Repetition* helps to strengthen the impression that something has made. That is why actors often repeat their lines to themselves several times so that they know not only what they have to say but when they have to say it. The greater the detail in which we have to remember things, the more repetitions we will usually require.
- *Writing things down* reinforces them. Look up a new telephone number in a directory and dial it. Very often you get so far through the number and then have to look at the directory again to complete it. Alternatively, look up a number in a telephone directory and write it down before you dial it. Almost certainly you will be able to complete dialling it without having to refer to it again.

- We remember information better if we *use* it. The telephone numbers we remember most readily are those we use most. The number we are most likely to forget is our own, because we very rarely need to use it.
- We remember things better if we have discussed them with others. *Discussion* is a very powerful reinforcing agent. We should seize upon opportunities for talking over with others the information we wish to remember. Most of us will have had the experience of attending meetings which discuss some items and pass over others quickly. It is nearly always the items where discussion has taken place where the greatest memory of them occurs. Asking ourselves questions or having others ask them helps to strengthen the impression that something makes. That is why the 'self-recitation' referred to above is such an effective technique.
- In addition to reinforcing information, we need to provide ourselves with '*triggers*' which will prompt the recall of the material we require. Self-recitation will also do this for us. Further triggers can be provided by using the techniques of *mnemonics*.

Mnemonics is a term which covers not only the study of memory, but also a range of well-tried and tested techniques for increasing our chances of remembering things. Some of the techniques have been in use for over two thousand years, which makes it all the more surprising that they do not find a place in our educational curriculum. A simple mnemonic may be based on *alliteration* or the repetition of a sound. 'Warm wet winters with westerly winds' as a reminder of the Mediterranean winter climate is an example.

Acronyms help us to remember. HOMES is a useful way of remembering the names of the Great Lakes in the USA – Huron, Ontario, Michigan, Erie and Superior. SHAPE – Supreme Headquarters Allied Powers Europe – is another one that older readers may remember.

Acrostics (using the initial letters of the words to remember to form a more readily recalled phrase or saying) can help. You can remember the colours of the rainbow or spectrum with the statement 'Richard of York gave battle in vain' – red, orange, yellow, green, blue, indigo, violet. Many of us may recall using a statement like 'Every good boy deserves favour' to remember the notes on the lines of a musical scale and FACE for the notes in the spaces in between.

Rhymes can be used, too. You may recall Rudyard Kipling's little rhyme about his 'serving men':

> I keep six honest serving men
> They taught me all I knew
> Their names are WHAT? and WHY? and WHEN?
> And HOW? and WHERE? and WHO?

These simple questions are also known as 'the journalist's questions', because they help to ensure that a writer has covered all the angles of a story. You might find it useful to run through them every time you try self-recitation. They will give you a better chance of recalling all the information you require.

In addition to these mnemonic techniques, there are four main mnemonic systems you may like to try:

- The system of '*loci*', or places. This technique has been traced back to at least 500 BC, when Greek and Roman orators used it to remember their speeches. They would have a mental picture of their villa or of a well-known public building and they would have a pre-determined route through it. They would make an association between a point they wanted to make and something in one of the rooms. Then, as they made their speech, they would mentally move from room to room, recalling their points in the right sequence as they went. The loci system works well because places provide very strong association links. We remember familiar places in great detail and the same place can provide the possibility for making several associations without repetition.

- The second system is usually called the '*link*' system. This is simply because it is once again based on associations which are linked together to form patterns or stories. The second way of carrying out the exercise in the Review section above is an example of the link system at work.

- The '*peg*' system. It is based on certain set associations linked to numbers, for example:

One = Bun	Four = Door
Two = Shoe	Five = Hive
Three = Tree	Six = Sticks

Seven = Heaven		Nine = Wine	
Eight = Gate		Ten = Hen	

This system is suitable for things like shopping lists, list of people's names at a party or any collection of unrelated pieces of information. Suppose you had to buy a water set, an ashtray and a watch. You may have many more items, but these will serve to illustrate the use of the technique. The first item was a water set so we link it to the number one and we may have a mental picture of a water set filled not with water but with buns. This is an odd image and may help to strengthen the impression made. The second item was an ashtray, so we may picture a shoe being used as an ashtray. This is a fairly revolting image for most people and this may strengthen its impression. The third item was a watch, so we may picture a tree with watches hanging from it rather than fruit. This surrealist image again may be stronger than something more mundane. It has to be said, however, that evidence available suggests that whilst the ridiculous, the revolting and the surreal may produce strong images, even quite ordinary, everyday associations greatly increase the chances of remembering things. You do not have to be a wildly bohemian individual with a warped sense of humour to build up your memory skills.

- The last system, and the 'grandaddy' of them all in terms of complexity, is the '*phonetic*' system. This is again based on numbers. Numbers are equated with letters and the letters are chosen because they represent the most common consonant sounds in English. The system looks like this:

Number	*Sound Equivalent*	*Way of Remembering Each One*
1	t, th or d	A 't' has a single downward stroke
2	n	Two downward strokes
3	m	Three downward strokes
4	r	Four ends in an 'r' sound, as in several languages
5	l	Latin for fifty is 'l'; drop the 0
6	g	6 upside down looks like 'g'
7	c or k	A 'k' can be written with two 7s back to back
8	f, v	'f' can be written to look like 8

9	b, p	9 upside down looks like 'b'
0	s or z	The last number is the last sound in the alphabet (mnemonics does not recognise the mathematical convention of putting 0 first!)

Once you have memorised all of this so well that numbers are instantly letters or sounds, you make associations between what you wish to remember and double-digit numbers, starting at 00 (which would perhaps be 'ss'). Possible association words for this combination would be 'seas', 'shoes', 'sees', 'sews', 'soars' and 'sues'. It is a complicated system, but its use goes back to the eighteenth century and those who use it claim it is very effective for mastering things quickly like vocabulary lists in foreign languages. The TV magician, Paul Daniels, has claimed on one of his programmes that the system helps him to remember up to 10,000 different items at once and he has used it to learn a working vocabulary of 800 Spanish words in a week.

Those who wish to pursue their knowledge and understanding of the phonetic technique, and indeed any of the other techniques described here, should read the starred book on memory in the Further Reading list at the back of the book.

Evaluation

Here is a list of the fifty states of the USA for you to memorise. They are in alphabetical order and you may like to try the link system. Begin with Alabama. An association for this might be the song 'I'm Alabammy Bound'. You might picture a little train on its way to Alabama, rather like the one in the Walt Disney film, *Dumbo*. The second one is Alaska. You might picture the dessert, Baked Alaska. You now begin to link the associations together, so you may have a mental picture of a trainload of Baked Alaska on its way to Alabama. Now you carry on from there:

Alabama Alaska Arizona Arkansas California Colorado Connecticut Delaware Florida Georgia Hawaii Idaho Illinois Indiana Iowa Kansas Kentucky Louisiana Maine Maryland Massachusetts Michigan Minnesota Mississippi Missouri Montana Nebraska Nevada New Hampshire

New Jersey New Mexico New York North Carolina North Dakota Ohio Oklahoma Oregon Pennsylvania Rhode Island South Carolina South Dakota Tennessee Texas Utah Vermont Virginia Washington West Virginia Wisconsin Wyoming

Wait for three days and then see if you can recall the names of all 50 states. If you have used the link system, you should find that you can still recall them in any order – from first to last, from last to first, from the middle outwards. Once you have your story, the names of the states almost seem to remember themselves. If you prefer, you can try this exercise with any similar list of items which you feel is of more relevance to you.

Ongoing

Activities which will promote the development of a more efficient memory are:

- Regular use of self-recitation, especially if you combine it with another technique known as '*mind-mapping*'. This involves using the journalist's questions (see page 39) to note down information, not in the more familiar form of a list, but radiating out from a central point. This permits a much freer and unfettered exploration of the topic and you do not become tied to a particular way of organising the information at too early a stage.

- Regular exercise in remembering things, using whichever of the techniques described in this chapter you find works best for you. You may need to experiment a little before these become completely clear.

- Identify the date of the first Monday in each month for the current (or, if you prefer, next) year. Take the numbers and, using the phonetic system, convert them to letters and then devise a word or phrase or mental picture which will help you to remember them. Doing this gives you a permanent mental calendar for the year so that, even if you do not have your diary with you, you will always know on which day of the week a date falls (assuming you can count up to seven), which months have five Mondays (or Fridays or any other day) and so on. For example, 1991 gave the following sequence (in 3-month blocks):

744 – 163 – 152 – 741

Converted into letters, using the phonetic system, these become:

CRR – TGM – TLN – CRN

Possible words for the first group are 'carry', 'carer', 'career' and 'curry'.

Possible phrases for the second group are 'the game' or 'the gum'.

Possibilities for the third group are 'to lone', 'talon', and 'tiling'.

Possible words for the fourth group are 'corn', 'crown', 'croon', and 'crayon'.

From this selection, you might pick 'carry', 'the gum', 'to lone', and 'crown'. Your sentence to remember might be 'Carry the gum to lone crown'. A mental picture of yourself taking some chewing gum to a rather sad looking king on a throne. Concentrate on the king's crown – perhaps it is sitting on his head at an odd angle – otherwise you might substitute king for crown when you come to remember your mnemonic! You could, of course, if you prefer, picture a queen on a throne, although in children's stories queens are not traditionally figures of fun as kings often are.

You might like to work out a similar mnemonic method for memorising the calendar for 1992 or 1993 or any other year you choose.

Completion checklist

At the end of this chapter you should be able to answer the following questions:

1 What have surgeons in the United States discovered about memory?
2 At what point do we experience most difficulties with memory?
3 How many of the characteristics which information should possess for greater ease of remembering can you list?
4 What does the mnemonic ALP stand for?

5 What does the acronym HOMES stand for?
6 Who or what were Kipling's 'serving men'?
7 What are the names of the four main mnemonic systems?

Conclusion

You should find that carrying out the exercises in this chapter and regularly putting your chosen mnemonic techniques into practice is not only useful, but fun as well. There is a great deal of satisfaction to be had just from the simple act of readily recalling things on demand. If you have information to remember for an important meeting or for an examination, you should find the techniques particularly useful.

Over a period of time, the benefits of improving your memory skills can be incalculable. It does require the investment of some time and effort, but nothing worthwhile was ever achieved without some effort. The important thing is to pace yourself and to avoid trying to achieve too much too soon. Do it gradually and in comfortable steps and stages and you will still get there.

Now we turn our attention to techniques of effective learning.

Review what you have learned from this chapter before you go to sleep tonight.

6

EFFECTIVE LEARNING

Perhaps the most surprising omission of all is that we are not taught at school how to learn. Research over many years has shown that there are strategies to use which make learning easier and more effective. Yet very few schools and colleges even now provide training in the use of these strategies. As a result, many people use ineffective methods of learning which are both time-consuming and hard work. In this chapter, we shall see how easy it is to remedy the situation.

You can carry out most activities more successfully if you approach them purposefully and systematically. This principle underlies most of the training in this book, but it is particularly true for techniques of learning. It does not matter whether you wish to learn in order to pass examinations or study documents in order to play a more effective part in a discussion or meeting. Success is more likely when you know your precise objectives and follow a plan to reach them.

Review

Describe the study strategy you currently use.

Do not read on until you have completed this task.

The chances are that you had nothing to write because you have no strategy to describe, for the reasons already outlined. Those who did have a strategy to describe should compare it with the one explained in this chapter to see if it measures up to what is known about effective study strategies.

Problems

There are so many problems faced by the ineffective learner that probably the simplest thing to do is to list them:

- The lack of a sense of purpose;
- Failure to use time efficiently;
- Lack of planning;
- Failure to use a study strategy;
- Slow reading;
- Lack of skill in notemaking;
- Poor preparation for studying;
- Failure to revise continuously and progressively;
- Failure to discuss with others the material to be learned;
- Ignoring the effects of physical and mental health on the ability to learn effectively;
- Ignoring the effects of environmental factors upon learning;
- Poor concentration;
- Lack of motivation;
- Being too much discouraged by failure.

Most of these problems will be solved by the contents of this chapter. Some will be solved by work in other chapters, for instance, those on reading and time management.

With so many hurdles to overcome, it will take more than one short chapter to surmount all of them.

Objectives

The basic objectives you should have (though you should, of course, add some specific objectives of your own to the list) are:

- Using an effective strategy to achieve mastery of a subject or skill;
- Performing successfully in a situation in which one's knowledge or abilities are being tested;
- Planning learning time and work more efficiently;
- Reading more efficiently for study purposes;
- Making effective notes and summaries of information and ideas.

Methods

The first step to take towards effective learning is to be clear about your objectives. Unless you know where you are going, there is not much chance of your getting there. It is even worth writing down your objectives, so that you can check later to see if you have achieved them.

Whatever the nature of the learning that has to be done, there will usually be a limited amount of time available before you are confronted with an examination of some kind. Not all of this time will be available for study because other activities, like eating, sleeping and travelling will also make demands upon it. Unless you calculate as early as possible how much time you can use for a study task, you will be in great danger of wasting a large proportion of it. Then you will have to make up the deficit by foregoing sleep or leisure activities.

Once you know how much time you have available for a learning task, you need to draw up a plan for using it. If the time has to be broken up to fit in with other activities, it is better, for instance, if learning sessions allow for the completion of at least a single chapter of a book or section of a report. It is useful to set down not only the total time available, but how much you will spend on each part of the task. Where possible, you should give the times of day you will devote to the studying. The plan is not something to stick to rigidly come what may, it is simply a method of making better use of time and effort. If you have to depart from it for whatever reason, then you have to depart from it. The fact that you make changes to a plan does not render it useless. In fact, it serves to emphasise the need for careful planning. Someone without a learning plan at all will waste a lot more time than someone who does have one.

Clear objectives and a plan for action provide a good basis for the use of a systematic study strategy. When it comes to the next step, actually carrying out the studying, method is even more important. In recent years, increasing attention has been given to identifying effective study methods and I have devised one with the mnemonic title PINCER, which I suppose conveys the connotation of getting to grips with a subject. The stages of the method are as follows:

- **Prepare**: Survey the available information and material generally to decide the amount of study time and effort you are likely to require. Assess the purposes of your studying and define what you hope to achieve by it. Assess your prior knowledge and experience that will be relevant. Identify any gaps, either in your prior knowledge or in the material to hand which you must fill before you can proceed.
- **Inspect**: Preview the facts and the material in some detail. Establish the pattern of organisation of the information, the general outline of the points to be covered and identify those parts which you anticipate will give greatest difficulty in understanding. Read the material thoroughly.
- **Note**: Make your own summaries of the main points, omitting points of secondary or minor importance. In these summaries, use mind-mapping and self-recitation to help in recalling the information (see Chapter 5 for an explanation of these techniques).
- **Consider and Evaluate**: Immediately after completing each study session (or as soon afterwards as possible) assess the value and overall significance of what you have learned. Make sure you understand thoroughly each stage and study again or seek advice if you do not. Set aside some time in which you can simply let the information mull over in the mind. This is a kind of 'incubation period' which has the effect of giving the brain time to draw its conclusions and generally evaluate the material more reliably.
- **Revise**: Do this the same day for the first revision. Afterwards revise continuously and progressively (that is, look quickly back over previous revisions at each revision session to check that no holes have appeared in the fabric of your knowledge) until you have mastered the information or are at least as sufficiently familiar with it as your purposes in studying require you to be.

There is no reason, of course, why you should not devise your own system of steps to be followed that meets your requirements more closely than the above method may. There is no single method that is superior to all others. The test lies in the actual usage of a method and you should not slavishly follow PINCER if a modification or a completely different approach will suit you better. The point to remember is that almost any study method will produce better results than no method at all.

The next chapter deals in more detail with reading, but it will be useful at this point to say a little about the special requirements of study reading. The first point is that it *takes time.* There are no short-cuts and no easy ways if you are to master the material effectively. That is not to say that you cannot use rapid reading and skimming techniques at certain stages of the study process. But if material is difficult to understand and if you have to comprehend it in detail and in depth, you can only really save time through the use of the kind of systematic approach outlined above. In other words, you increase speed in handling by avoiding the wastage of time in studying inessentials.

Apart from being generally slow and methodical, study reading also requires a high level of concentration. You should not read materials in conditions in which distractions are likely, if this can be avoided in any way. Good concentration is not achieved by effort. It comes from an environment in which the mind can give its whole attention to the task facing it.

Quiet is necessary and those who maintain that they can study better when the radio is blaring out pop music deceive no one but themselves. Music may help but it must not intrude on thinking about the study material. It should only provide a background and perhaps mask some of those small noises that can be very distracting in conditions of almost total silence.

Where possible, discuss your reading with others who are engaged in the same task. Discussion is probably one of the most pleasant and yet, very often, the least practised way of testing your comprehension of material and of having your understanding either challenged or confirmed by others.

To be an effective learner you must be a flexible reader. You should not devote time and effort to reading matter regardless of its importance or relevance to you. Skim materials quickly when selecting those you will study. Skim or read rapidly when dealing with background materials.

You will do a small proportion of your reading relatively slowly because it presents either entirely new material or is more difficult for some other reason. Essential materials will be read, re-read and notes made based upon them. You will, in fact, do most of your reading with a pen and notepad to hand, even when you are skimming or reading rapidly, for you will never know when you may have to note something in writing to ensure that you remember it.

The characteristics of the effective learner can be summarised as follows. He or she:

- Has clearly defined objectives;
- Plans use of time carefully;
- Prepares a study plan and tries to keep to it;
- Follows a systematic study method;
- Is a flexible reader;
- Makes accurate, brief notes in his or her own words;
- Prepares for test situations in good time;
- Revises continuously and progressively;
- Discusses materials with others whenever opportunities occur;
- Realises the importance of good physical and mental health;
- Chooses appropriate environments for learning;
- Concentrates easily and well;
- Is highly motivated to learn.

Evaluation

Here is a little test to help you to decide how well you have understood the principles of effective learning:

1 Before a student begins to study he or she must:
   a) discuss what is to be learned with others
   b) define objectives
   c) set aside a regular time for study each day
   d) have plenty of time for revision

2 Successful students tend to be:
   a) slow readers
   b) average readers
   c) flexible readers
   d) fast readers

3 A student needs:
   a) very little sleep
   b) good mental and physical health
   c) more sleep than average
   d) frequent meals

4 A good notemaker should be able to:
   a) make concise, accurate notes
   b) write down a little more than will be needed
   c) write down as much as possible in the time available
   d) write down about half of whatever the material contains

5 The fourth step in the PINCER study strategy is:
   a) Prepare
   b) Revise
   c) Consider and Evaluate
   d) Inspect

6 Revision should be:
   a) left until the last minute
   b) carried out continuously and progressively
   c) carried out every weekend
   d) unnecessary if the studying has been done properly

See page 188 for the answers to these questions.

Ongoing

Activities which will help to improve the development of effective learning include:

- Regular practice in setting objectives for study;
- Regular practice in self-recitation;
- Regular practice in mind-mapping;
- Regular use of a study strategy like PINCER;
- Continuous and progressive revision.

Completion checklist

At the end of this chapter you should be able to answer the following questions:

1 How many of the problems faced by the ineffective learner can you list?
2 What are the five stages in the PINCER study strategy?
3 When should you first revise what you have learned?
4 Why should you discuss what you study with others?
5 How many of the characteristics of the effective learner can you list?
6 What is 'self-recitation'?
7 What is 'mind-mapping'?

Conclusion

Being able to learn effectively is a fundamental skill. You will find that if you put all the advice and guidance given in this chapter into practice not only will it make studying the other chapters in this book easier, it will also make learning generally easier, more productive and even more enjoyable. There is no reason at all why learning should be thought of as being unpleasant drudgery through which you put yourself in the hope of some kind of reward at a later date. There is every reason why it should be a richly rewarding and satisfying activity in its own right.

Review what you have learned from this chapter before you go to sleep tonight.

7

EFFICIENT READING

Most of us are taught how to read in primary school and that is the last instruction we receive in reading techniques. It seems that we are expected to know how to develop our reading skills on our own. As an inevitable consequence most of us are slow and inefficient readers who read for most purposes at a speed of about 200–250 words per minute (wpm). This is not much faster than we read aloud. Radio talks are scripted at 150 wpm and those are hardly rushed affairs. Television newscasts are a little brisker at 3 words a second or 180 wpm. The astronomer Patrick Moore may be faster than that, but he is very much the exception.

Can anything be done about this? Or are we condemned to reading slowly and not very well? Fortunately, research dating back to the 1870s indicates that it is possible for many people to speed up their reading without any adverse effects upon comprehension. A large number of readers find that faster reading actually gives them better comprehension. The means by which increases in speed can be achieved are not difficult to master and we shall look at a number of them in this chapter. Once again, it will be for you to decide which methods work best in your own case.

Review

For this exercise you will need a stopwatch or a watch with a timer facility or, at the very least, a watch with a second hand and clearly marked minutes on its face. The instructions below are for stop-watches and timers. If you only have a watch with a second hand, you will need to begin reading at the beginning of a minute and to make a note of the time you start. When you have finished reading, you will need to note the time again and subtract the earlier time from it to find out how long you took to read the passage. You will also need a pen or pencil to take the comprehension test which follows the passage. Select a time and place which will ensure that you are not interrupted during the exercise. Follow the instructions carefully.

Read the following passage once only as quickly as you feel you can take it in. Right from the start of the chapter we are trying to find out how quickly you can read at present. We shall explore ways of increasing this speed with the same or better comprehension.

Begin reading and begin timing **NOW**.

How To Be a Good Judge

We are all judges. We make judgments about all sorts of things every day. For the most part, we make these judgments with little or no regard for the simple scientific principles of observation, hypothesis, testing and evaluation. They are the product of a complex mixture of prejudice, naked self-interest and instinct. The amazing thing is not so much that this approach works reasonably well as that it works at all. But we do get by and no matter how odd our attitudes and opinions may be on a wide range of issues, the wheels keep turning and life is lived.

But is it, after all, good enough? Should we not give a little more time and attention to how we make judgments and see if we cannot improve our skill in making them? We know that the answer to the first question is that it is not good enough and to the second that we should and can find ways of making sounder judgments. So how should we go about seeking improvements?

One way would be to attend a short course of training. There are not many of these to be had, but some colleges do offer them. The main advantage in attending is that you become a member of a group. The group is an exacting and accurate testing ground for judgments, for members of the group soon expose those that will not stand up to close examination. If the group carries out the process with a certain amount of give-and-take and if there is a sympathetic and understanding tutor, enjoyment as well as improved skill in making judgments should result.

Typically, a course will consist of eight sessions, probably at weekly intervals, though two-day courses are possible (an arrangement which enables them to be fitted into programmes of management training in business and industry). The pattern of organisation of courses can vary to suit group needs, but one which meets a wide variety of needs follows the pattern described below.

The first three sessions of the course are occupied by exercises in 'seeing' in which group members are confronted with pictures, photographs or short films. They are then, as a piece of individual work, asked to respond in writing to what they have seen. They may be asked to list the differences between two pictures, or to decide what a photograph shows, or give their reactions to a film.

This individual work may not actually be used in the subsequent group discussion of the material, but it serves as an opportunity for group members to organise their responses into some kind of form and this tends to make discussion easier and more productive. It soon becomes clear that different people have seen different things in the material and have responded in different ways. Discussion provides an arena in which interpretations can be examined and analysed. Judgments are challenged and defended and in the process are often modified.

The fourth session centres round a consideration of 'language' and its effect on our ability to make accurate judgments. Group members respond individually again, this time to a passage which contains words like 'normal' and 'average' and then discuss what they have understood by these words.

For the fifth session, the group members are asked to write a short essay on 'Classification'. This is used as a basis for discussion on how we classify our knowledge and experience and on the validity of the labels and compartments we use.

An article or a paper from a scientific or technical journal is used in the next session as a basis for a discussion on 'The evaluation of evidence'. The group now confronts the central problem and uses what it has learned from previous sessions to reach conclusions about the approaches which are most likely to result in sound judgments.

The seventh session is concerned with a major issue in much scientific, technical and management thinking, 'causation'. A problem has arisen or a new situation is encountered and before it can be effectively dealt with an assessment of its causes must be made. It is one of the key areas of judgment making. The stimulus for the discussion in this session is an article on the causes of a problem or situation in which the group members are involved.

The final session of the course is spent in a review of what the group has learned. Individual and general conclusions can be discussed and evaluated.

Courses like this have a number of effects on their participants. Generally, group members become more objective and more flexible in their behaviour. Specifically, when compared to control groups, those who had attended the courses tended to discriminate better between facts and conclusions. They tended to draw fewer false conclusions, to consider more than one solution to a problem and to be less adversely influenced in their approach to a problem by their experience of a preceding one.

The organisation of the course undoubtedly plays a significant part in making results like these possible. The size of groups is kept between eight and twelve members and participants sit facing each other in a rough circle. The discussions are taped and can be used for a variety of purposes, for instance, to allow a group to reconsider part of its deliberations or to allow boisterous groups to hear quieter ones (and vice versa) so that they can learn to operate effectively. The pattern of each session is usually: stimulus (a picture, photograph, film, etc.); individual response (in writing); free group discussion (to compare reactions to the stimulus); and conclusion (a rounding off, but not a total summary, of the discussion). The emphasis throughout the course is on requiring group members to distinguish between facts, inferences and conclusions.

The results which courses like this have produced would seem to be a powerful argument for their general introduction into the educational system. They would also appear to have potentially great benefits for many adults in a wide variety of business and industrial occupations, especially those who are, or aspire to become, supervisors and managers.

(*1014 words*)

Make a note of the time you have taken, then answer the following questions, selecting the most suitable option in each case.

Comprehension test

Recall

1 The first principle of the scientific method of making judgments is:
a) observation
b) evaluation
c) testing
d) hypothesis

2 The first three sessions of the course are occupied by exercises in:
a) classification
b) seeing
c) photography
d) film-making

3 A major issue in much scientific and technical thinking is:
a) classification
b) interpretation
c) causation
d) confrontation

4 One benefit of the course has been found to be:
a) more patience in listening to opposing viewpoints
b) a tendency to draw fewer false conclusions
c) an improvement in the use of language
d) a greater awareness of the importance of science

5 The emphasis throughout the course is on requiring group members to:
a) reach firm conclusions about the stimulus material
b) express themselves clearly and concisely
c) distinguish between facts, inferences and opinions
d) use the principles of the scientific method systematically

Interpretation

6 The tone of the comment 'The amazing thing is not so much that this approach works reasonably well as that it works at all',

made in relation to our tendency to make judgments without regard to simple scientific principles, is:
a) ironic
b) scathing
c) nostalgic
d) excitable

7 A person who was highly sensitive to criticism would probably find the course:
a) shocking
b) enjoyable
c) upsetting
d) satisfying

8 Judgments are often modified in the course of discussion because:
a) they have been shown to be false
b) people do not like to offend others
c) the tutor will point out deficiencies
d) people just like to change their minds

9 It is useful to discuss what people understand by the words 'normal' and 'average' because:
a) people often do not know what they mean
b) they are words in daily use
c) they are difficult words to understand
d) they are capable of carrying several meanings

10 The main point made by the passage may be said to be:
a) people should discuss problems before reaching judgments
b) judgments should be based upon scientific principles
c) prejudice hinders the making of judgments
d) people can learn to make better judgments

See page 189 for the answers to these questions.

Obtain your speed from the table on page 188.

Problems

The main problems of the inefficient reader are:

- **Regression.** Inefficient readers go back frequently to read things a second time, or even more often, because they feel that they have not taken in the meaning.

- **A narrow eye span.** As the eye moves along a line of print, it moves in a series of jerky movements, usually one word at a time. This is because the eye can only read when focused on the material and therefore stationary. Look at a word on a line and, without moving your eyes, see how many words you can also read on either side and in the lines above and below. This is your eye span or area of close focus vision.

- **Low speed of perception.** That is to say, the eye spends longer at each fixation point before moving on. In a fast reader the time is about 0.25 of a second. In an inefficient or slow reader, it is about 0.35 of a second.

- **Lack of rhythm in eye movements.** If there are frequent regressions and if the movements are small (word by word), the process is bound to be less rhythmic than if the fixations are more widely spaced and there is little or no regression.

- **Tendency to read everything slowly.** This is simply because inefficient readers usually have no choice but to read slowly, since they have never learned to do anything else.

- **Vocalisation or subvocalisation.** Vocalisation is a technical term for reading aloud. Some people are unable to read silently. Subvocalisation is harder to define, but perhaps the best way is to say that it is 'reading aloud silently', a mental articulation of every word. It tends to become less noticeable once reading speeds rise above about 300 wpm.

- **Lack of purpose in reading.** The inefficient reader often fails to define purpose and clarify expectations before reading. This lack of drive also contributes to slowness of approach.

- **Tension when reading under pressure.** Because reading takes so long, the slow reader finds that 'reading against the clock' (which is often necessary when, say, someone circulates papers without warning at a meeting and those present have to make decisions quickly) causes a rapid build-up of tension, which further inhibits the effectiveness of the reading.

- **Poor anticipation.** The inefficient reader cannot anticipate the nature of subsequent material when reading. As in the use of any skill, the person who can see the direction in which things are heading before they actually happen has an advantage.

- **Concentration.** The slow reader lacks concentration except for short periods. Concentration often improves with speed, if only because when you do anything faster, like driving a car, you have to concentrate more.

- **Retention.** The poor reader finds it difficult to retain much information for very long once they have finished reading. This may be in part due to a lack of knowledge of some of the techniques of mnemonics which we covered in Chapter 5.

- **Vocabulary.** The inefficient reader often has a rather limited vocabulary. This is perhaps a natural consequence of slowness. If you are slow, you cannot read as much in a given time, which makes it less likely that you will encounter many new words. Also the poor reader tends to read only what he or she has to read, which is a further narrowing factor.

- **Lack of a critical approach.** Poor readers tend to accept what is in print at face value because they have never had training of the kind described in the exercise above nor in techniques of critical reading of the kind explained later in this chapter.

- **Limited general background of knowledge and experience.** If you are a slow reader who only reads when it is unavoidable, this is bound to have a limiting effect on your range of knowledge and experience.

Objectives

The basic objectives you should have (though you should, of course, add more specific objectives of your own to the list) are:

- Doubling your reading speed (as shown by the exercise in the Review section above);
- Increasing your comprehension score by at least 10 per cent (unless you scored 10 out of 10);
- Increasing flexibility in dealing with reading materials by using a flexible reading strategy (some will be described in this chapter);
- Becoming a more critical reader by using a method like the one described in this chapter;
- Reading more widely by, for example, reading at least one book a month on a subject that you would otherwise not have read about.

Methods

The first thing to do before embarking upon a programme of reading skills development is to have your eyes tested. Where tests have been carried out on people before they began a course in reading efficiency, typical findings have been that, of those who were not wearing spectacles, about 30 per cent should have been. It has also been found that, of those who were wearing spectacles, about 30 per cent again needed new ones. If you have not had an eye test in the last two years, you may find it helpful to have one. Even if spectacles, or new ones, only give a slightly better contrast between the print and the paper, they will make reading an easier task. If it becomes easier, it will also become a little faster. You might as well have the benefit of this improvement.

Improvement in any skill, and reading is no exception, is easier to achieve if the participant brings to the process at least four basic attitudes and approaches:

- You are more likely to improve if you *want* to improve. Motivation need not be fanatical – you do not have to devote the rest of your life to reading improvement – but it will help if you actively want to improve.

- You are more likely to improve if you feel you *can* improve. Confidence may come from asking yourself when you last had training in reading techniques. If this was indeed, as suggested at the beginning of this chapter, in primary school, there is almost bound to be a training gap between what you have done and what you could have done which should suggest to you that some improvement at least should be possible.
- It will help if you consciously *try* to improve. Effort should not be excessive, however, because you can try too hard. A reasonable effort is all that is required. Every time you do a practice exercise of the kind suggested below you should, as athletes do, try for a new 'personal best' performance every time.
- You should also persist with your *practice*. Once you know what to do in any skill, and reading is no exception, it is practice which makes perfect. Once you have started, you have to finish. It takes work to improve any skill, but if you select materials you find interesting, it will not become a chore.

Every time you do a reading exercise of the kind described at the end of this chapter you should set yourself a target time for the reading, based upon your previous achievements, which will require a slightly higher speed than your best so far. You should also set a target of a slightly better comprehension score. You will not always achieve your targets, but you are more likely to do so if they are there than if they are not. You might also try setting time limits for other kinds of exercises based on your previous results. If it takes you twenty minutes to read your evening newspaper, for instance, set a target of nineteen minutes, then eighteen and so on until no further improvement is possible. You are aiming to double your reading speed, but expect this to take about six weeks or so of practice. Some people can do it in a week or less, but a gradual improvement will probably be a more solid one that is easier to maintain.

You will need regular feedback on your performance if you are to improve. Every time you do a reading exercise it must be timed, tested and recorded as you did in the Review above. It does not count as practice if you simply pick something up and start reading it and do not test yourself afterwards. Subjective impressions of the passage of time are notoriously unreliable, as in the saying, 'Doesn't the time pass quickly when you're having fun?' Conversely, if nothing much is happening, time seems to drag. You may think you have read something faster, but you will not know unless you time it. Much the same thing applies to impressions of the quality of comprehension as well, so test them both.

Those are some of the easier and more straightforward things you can do to lay a basis for your reading skill to improve. Since they are easy you might as well benefit from them. But there are many other techniques you can use and we will now look at them. Give each one a fair trial before you make your mind up as to whether to incorporate it into your personal approach to reading. Don't make your mind up after a single exercise. Things that do not work the first time may well begin to click into place after three or four attempts. Each one has considerable support in the research that has been done into reading over the years.

Every time you do a practice exercise, do not go back to read something a second time. No regression, to use the technical term. You will find that it helps if you use a postcard to cover up the material line by line as you read it, thus preventing regression. Keep the postcard moving. Do not allow it to stop. Do not allow it to go back. And do not have it following you along about three lines behind where you actually are just in case you are tempted to regress. Research shows that where people are put into a situation in which it is impossible to regress – a paragraph is usually projected on to a screen and then a shutter moves down at a set speed to cover it up – the loss of comprehension is on average no more than between 3 and 7 per cent and even that is recovered with a little practice. In other words, research indicates that we do not need most regressions; we can learn to do without them. But you have to try first. It won't happen simply because you say to yourself, 'No regression'. The barrier of the postcard has to be there at first to prevent it.

Once you can maintain speeds in excess of 300 wpm on most kinds of material, then you can begin to discard the postcard and perhaps use your hand or a pen to nudge you along. The ideal position to progress to is one where you move a pencil or a pen down the margin as a pacing aid. This means the pencil or pen is always in position to mark something of interest or importance. It is also there to put a little question mark in the margin if you come across something you do not understand. Then, if you get to the end and you still do not understand what was being said, you can 'regress' to the precise point in the text where the problem was and do not have to go looking for it. This kind of regression, where it is necessary, is more effective than going back immediately you have encountered a problem. Regress straightaway and you are trying to solve a problem with an incomplete picture of the context. Go to the end before going back and at least you then have a knowledge of what is there and what is not when you try to solve the problem. You can bring an awareness of the total context to bear on the passage.

As you read, try to identify how many pauses or fixations you make along the line. It should not be too difficult to do this because, in reading, the eyes are actually stationary for between 93 and 95 per cent of the time. The time taken up by the movements from one fixation point to the next is therefore very small. Once you know how many pauses you make, try to reduce the number. Try to take the material in in terms of *groups* of words rather than single words. 'The quick brown fox jumps over the lazy dog' contains nine words, or nine fixations. But it contains only three groups: 'The quick brown fox – jumps over – the lazy dog'. If you find that trying to do this simply means you are moving your eyes but nothing registers, do not worry. Abandon it and simply concentrate on trying to read faster. A lot of people do find that it makes more sense to let the mechanics of the process look after themselves. Just trying will get you there and the change will take place from word-by-word reading to wordgroup-by-wordgroup reading quite without any conscious involvement on your part. It usually happens at about 300 wpm or so.

You may also find it helpful if you can get into a rhythm – along the line, back, along the next line, back, and so on – this will not only help to encourage fewer fixations per line, but will also help to counter any tendency to regress. Once you get into a rhythm, it is less easy to break it.

As you read, read for *meaning*. Do not try to 'spot questions'. In other words, don't try to store bits of information away on the off-chance that they might be required. That is reading like a squirrel, storing nuts away for a possible need in winter. Concentrate on understanding what is there and then, if you do understand it, it won't matter what questions are asked because you'll be able to answer them.

Be clear about your purpose in reading. You can use the self-recitation questions first encountered in Chapter 5 to help you here. You can ask these questions both before and after reading something. If you do that, they are very likely to be in mind as you read. Consider what you are doing when you ask them. Ask the question 'What?' and you are automatically looking for information about events, actions, things, or to put it all in tabular form, this is what you are doing:

Question	**Looking for Information About**
What?	Events, actions, things
Why?	Reasons, conclusions, deductions, inferences, implications, opinions
When?	Time
How?	Methods, processes
Where?	Place
Who?	People

When you think about it, there is very little information that you cannot classify under one or other of these headings. So, in asking them, you cover all the possibilities. You also give yourself things to do. This can be very useful with uninteresting material.

One of the problems with reading is that, like listening, it is a receptive skill. If you are not careful, receptive skills can become purely passive; you simply do not get involved. When this happens, comprehension suffers. You have to become actively involved to achieve maximum performance.

Reading efficiency is improved if, before you begin, you spend a few seconds just looking through to see what the contents are. This '*previewing*', as it is called, is used by a lot of naturally rapid and efficient readers. Theory has it that going through the material twice like this – preview and then read – is actually faster than reading it once. Reading something through only once has to be taken more slowly at first until you familiarise yourself with the subject. All the time you are moving into the unknown. Preview first and at least you have some idea of what to expect and whether it will be interesting or not, easy or difficult, relevant or not, and so on. You will also have some idea of how the writer has organised the material which will help in deciding where to look for what. The time this previewing takes should, of course, be included in the overall reading time. It should take about half a minute or less per thousand words.

When reading, you should exploit every opportunity to use the full range of the techniques or '*gears*' available to you. Gears is perhaps a more appropriate term to use when you are talking about speeds anyway. There are four gears in reading: studying, slow reading, rapid reading, and skimming.

Studying involves reading, re-reading, making notes and revising and it was covered in Chapter 6.

Slow reading is familiar to all of us. Speeds run from about 150 wpm up to about 300 wpm, or around twice the speed of reading aloud. Speeds lower than 150 wpm tend to cause more problems than they solve. For instance, you tend to forget what you have read at the top of a page by the time you get to the bottom, simply because it is so long since you were there. It becomes progressively more difficult to relate what you are reading now to what you have already read and to prepare yourself for what is to come. The whole process of comprehension becomes clogged up and does not work very well. An analogy can be drawn with a car engine. If it does not get a reasonable fuel flow, it starts to cough and splutter. Similarly, the brain if it does not get a reasonable information flow, does not work very well – though, unlike a car engine, it will hopefully not come to a complete stop as a result!

Rapid reading runs from about 300 wpm to about 800 wpm. This is the gear that is missing from many people's repertoires. This is the range we need to progress into to complete our armoury of techniques. If you follow the instruction and advice given in this chapter, it should not be long before you join the ranks of those who can read rapidly and efficiently.

Skimming is the fastest gear and involves allowing the eyes to break away from line by line movements and range more freely across and down the page. It works best if you have some key words or phrases to look for. At the very least, you should have the six self-recitation questions in mind. It is a useful technique for deciding what to read (previewing is a form of skimming) and what not to read. At its simplest, it gives an idea of how something is organised and that then makes a subsequent reading easier, faster and more productive.

Reading is more efficient if it is done systematically, using what is known as a *flexible reading strategy*. One such is **P2R** or preview – read – review. The idea is that you skim through something, then read it as quickly as your purpose in reading and the material itself will allow, and then skim through it quickly again to reinforce the impression that the important points have made. You can abandon the system at any point if you feel you have taken in all you need to and you can repeat any step as required. This means that you can use it very flexibly to meet the needs of a wide variety of situations.

When you read, you should use *context cues*. These are the words or phrases which tell you what the material is about, that is, key words. They are useful in skimming, as we have just seen, but they are also useful in reading generally. These important or key words and phrases 'cue you in', as it were, to the context in which things are being said. They are another method by which you can control the processing of the information more effectively.

You should always read critically. That is to say, you should take nothing in at face value. Even when reading quickly, you should approach the task with an air of healthy scepticism. Asking the questions 'What?', 'Why?' and 'How?' from the six self-recitation questions is a particularly useful thing to do.

Sometimes, rather than read something once only at a fairly slow speed, it is better to read it twice quickly. This can work very well, especially if the first reading concentrates on those parts which you can understand more easily and you put a question mark in the margin next to difficulties. On the second reading you can then concern yourself with the problem areas alone.

Using abstracts and digests can be a useful way of having some of your reading done by others. Remember Francis Bacon's advice in his essay, 'Of Studies':

> Some Bookes are to be Tasted, Others to be Swallowed, and Some Few to be Chewed and Digested: that is, some Bookes are to be read onely in Parts: Others to be read but not Curiously: and some Few are to be read wholly and with Diligence and Attention. Some Bookes also may be read by Deputy, and Extracts made of them by Others.

Sound advice on techniques of efficient reading from the seventeenth century!

Taking regular tests is a useful technique in its own right. Select material that is relevant to your needs or interests and time the reading of passages that are not too long. Test comprehension with a self-recitation test. Calculate speed by timing the reading and then estimate the number of words read by counting the words in ten lines, dividing by ten and multiplying by the number of lines read.

Divide the number of words read by the time taken in seconds and multiply by 60 to convert to wpm.

Alternatively, you can try exercises in one of the many books on reading efficiency that are available if you do not want to go to the trouble of setting your own tests or calculating your reading speed without the aid of a conversion table.

Finally, if you want to improve your reading skills, *practise, practise, practise*. As with any skill, once you know what to do, much of the rest is practice. Five or ten minutes a day is better than nothing. Half an hour a day is ideal. Keep it up until you are confident that you have exploited all the potential for improvement that you have.

Evaluation

After you have put the guidance and advice given in the Methods section into practice for about six weeks, read the following passage and answer the questions at the end.

Read the passage once only as quickly as you feel you can take it in.

Begin reading and begin timing **NOW**.

How To Make Learning Fun

The use of games and simulations as a training technique is by no means new. People have played war games for nearly five thousand years and have used them in training people in the arts and skills of strategy. But a resurgence of interest has occurred in recent years. Not only has renewed attention been given to war gaming, but also to business gaming and to the general extension of the use of games and simulations to many kinds of teaching and training. In geography teaching, for instance, and in the training of teachers, the techniques have become a standard feature.

The essential difference between a game and a simulation, though many would dispute that a clear line can be drawn, is that a game is competitive and is played according to certain rules, whereas a simulation merely sets out to re-create in the classroom a situation that the participants can expect to encounter outside or one from which general lessons can be learned. In practice, of course, some simulations, such as negotiations and bargaining procedures of various kinds, may be highly competitive and may even have fairly rigid rules of acceptable conduct.

It may seem, on the face of it, to be a fairly formidable task to plan and devise a game or simulation that will suit a particular purpose. But, provided the problem is approached systematically and certain basic rules are borne in mind, it is well within the capabilities of any teacher or trainer to prepare his or her own.

The first step is to define the objectives which you want to achieve. This should make it clear whether a game or simulation will be a suitable training method. They are best fitted for situations in which the aim is to show participants how a conflict functions or how people tend to behave in given circumstances. They are thus of greater relevance to work in the social studies and the humanities than to work in science and technology. They are of more use in teaching social and human relations skills than in teaching the factual content of a particular area of human knowledge. They are of more interest to the manager and the student who wishes to improve his or her linguistic and social skills than to the technical specialist or the industrial operative.

Once you have defined the objectives and they are within those that games and simulations can help in achieving, you have to decide the context within which the action will take place. The subject selected will largely dictate this and if, for instance, the aim is to develop skill in putting a case forward successfully, then the most appropriate context may be that of negotiation.

The next key question is to decide who will take part. The identities of the players will be largely determined by the context and the actual situation, but some selection will usually be possible. The number of active participants needs to be kept within reasonable limits or the situation will get out of hand.

You now have to define the structure of the simulation and make a decision on what each participant will try to achieve, from what point the simulation will begin, how much time to allow and how the moves are to be made. The simulation must progress and, if you select negotiation as the context, the moves may take the form of bids and counterbids with discussions and attempts by each side to persuade the other to make concessions until they reach a mutually acceptable settlement.

Other points which can call for decisions include the definition of what a round will be, what the attitudes of the players are to be, how much information each participant is to have about his or her own and others' roles before the simulation begins and how much other background information to give to the players. You will determine the answers to many of these questions by how much freedom of movement the players are to have and how large an element role-playing is to have in the simulation. The more scope there is for role-playing and for the role-players themselves to define their roles, the less structure and the fewer rules the simulation will need.

After the completion of the game or the simulation of the problem or situation being studied, you should have a period of evaluation in which the participants can assess what they have learned. It also provides an opportunity for the organiser to provide feedback and comment on the actions and reactions of the players. You can enhance the value of this if you make a sound or video recording of the proceedings. If such a recording can be made available for study and analysis by the group, the lessons learned from the simulation can be greatly increased.

Usually time for evaluation will be limited, but if it is not, you will have to judge when enough time has been spent on the 'inquest' and the group should begin to look forward again.

Relatively few studies have been made of the effectiveness of games and simulations as training methods, but there would appear to be few drawbacks in their use. One undoubtedly is the unwillingness of some people to take part in simulations which have a strong emphasis on role-playing. This is a little too close to 'acting' and that is a little too close to enjoying yourself rather than getting down to some useful work. The same Victorian ethic comes into play with games that have too strong an entertainment factor. Some people simply do not seem able to accept the idea that certain kinds of learning can be both easy and pleasurable.

For those who have no such inhibitions, games and simulations can help to provide a reasonably realistic framework in which effective learning can take place and mistakes can be made inexpensively. Mistakes made in real situations may teach as much, but would certainly cost more.

(995 words)

Make a note of the time you have taken, then answer the following questions, selecting the most suitable option in each case.

Comprehension test

Recall

1 The essential difference between a game and a simulation is that a game is:
a) shorter
b) longer
c) competitive
d) co-operative

2 In preparing a simulation, the first step is to:
a) decide who will play
b) define the objectives
c) work out the rules
d) determine the context in which the interaction will take place

3 The number of participants needs to be:
a) kept within reasonable limits
b) kept to a minimum
c) kept to a maximum
d) kept within strict limits

4 If there is more scope for role-playing, a simulation will need:
a) more rules
b) a complete set of rules
c) no rules at all
d) fewer rules

5 Mistakes made in real life compared with a simulation may teach:
a) nothing at all
b) more
c) less
d) as much

Interpretation

6 Negotitaions may be highly competitive because:
a) each side will be hostile to the other
b) each side will want to achieve the best outcome for itself
c) co-operation between the sides would defeat the whole purpose of the negotiations
d) it is human nature to be competitive

7 It may seem a formidable task to plan a simulation because:
a) it is a new training technique
b) considerable skill is needed
c) the reader may not have planned one before
d) the procedure for planning one is difficult to follow

8 A negotiating situation may help to improve skill in putting a case forward because:
a) more time can be allowed for preparation
b) participants will be able to observe cases being put forward
c) participants will themselves have to put their cases forward
d) there will be an opportunity to evaluate performance afterwards

9 A 'round' in a simulation may be defined as:
a) an amount of time
b) a sequence of operations
c) a sequence of moves
d) a number of games

10. A video recording of the progress of a simulation would be particularly useful because:
a) it would show others how to proceed
b) it would provide entertainment afterwards
c) people would see how they had themselves acted
d) it would provide a permanent record of the simulation

See page 189 for the answers to these questions.

Obtain your speed from the table on page 188.

Have you doubled your reading speed (as shown by the first exercise in this chapter) and increased your comprehension score by at least 10 per cent? If you have not, you should make a special effort to find the time to carry out some of the exercises described in the next section. You should remember that some people need more practice than others in order to achieve their objectives. Above all, do not be discouraged. Keep trying.

Ongoing

Activities which will help to continue the development of efficient reading techniques include:

- Read at least one book a month on a subject that interests you, but which you would not otherwise have read.
- Select an article every day from a journal which you know you ought to read, but which you feel you currently do not have time to read. Time the reading and test comprehension with a self-recitation test.
- Read a short 'News in Brief' item from a newspaper. Time the reading. When you have finished, put the item to one side. On a blank sheet of paper, see how many of the facts you can remember. Check accuracy by referring back to the original. Count the number of words. Divide that figure by the time taken in seconds and then multiply by 60 to convert to wpm.
- Read a feature article in a newspaper and time the reading. Put it to one side and then, on a blank sheet of paper, write down the main points made in the article. Restrict yourself to six at the most, for this is an exercise in selecting the most important points made. Estimate the length of the article by counting the number of words in a column inch and then multiplying that by the total length of the article in column inches. Check the selection of main points the day after the reading or ask someone else to check it for you.
- Practise P2R on at least one journal article or book chapter a week.
- Try moving away from using the postcard as a method of avoiding regression to using your hand as a barrier, then a pen (remembering not to skip back over it to look at text already read), and finally to using your pen or pencil as a pointer at the

right or left hand side margin. Keep the pointer moving just a little faster than you would really like. The pen or pencil is also then in position for any quick marks you wish to make in the margin to remind you where important points are or things you do not quite understand and may need to make a calculated regression to afterwards.

- Re-read the Methods section of this chapter every three months to make sure that you are still putting all the points into practice.
- Make a note of any new words you encounter in your reading. Look up the meanings in a dictionary and make a note of those, too. Try using the words in one or two sentences of your own construction. If you are not sure whether or not you have quite grasped the meanings, ask a sympathetic friend to check them for you.
- Practise skimming on one or more of the 'quality' Sunday newspapers to find articles of particular interest or relevance to you.
- Once a year, work through this chapter again and see if there is any further increase in speed or improvement in comprehension possible.

Completion checklist

At the end of this chapter you should be able to answer the following questions:

1 Within what speed range do most of us read?
2 How many problems of the inefficient reader can you list?
3 What is the first thing you should do before embarking upon a programme of reading skills development?
4 What four basic attitudes and approaches should you bring to the process?
5 What is 'previewing'?
6 What is P2R?
7 What is often more effective than reading something slowly once?
8 What was the final piece of advice given if you want to improve your reading skills?

Conclusion

It should be clear to you by now, and especially from some of the exercises in the Ongoing section, that reading improvement, like education itself, is a lifelong process. We can never truly exploit all our potential for improvement. Indeed, this is probably true for all the skills in this book.

Reading is such a fundamental skill in our highly technological, complex society that inevitably we have had to spend rather more time on it than usual. Now you are probably ready for a shorter chapter and one in which, by its very nature, the exercises will take you away from this book for a while. Let us see how we may improve our listening skills.

Review what you have learned from this chapter before you go to sleep tonight.

8

EFFICIENT LISTENING

No communication skill has been more neglected than listening. We receive almost no training in listening in our schools and colleges. Such little training as does occur takes place incidentally during training in oral expression. Yet our ability in aural comprehension probably provides us with the basis of most of our knowledge and awareness of the people and the world around us.

Review

How many different kinds of listening do you think there are? List them.

Do not read on until you have completed this exercise.

Afterwards, compare your list with the one that appears later in this section.

Problems

As we use the terms here, hearing is a passive, random, accidental activity: listening is active, purposeful and systematic. We hear all the sounds that there are to hear, waking or sleeping; we listen to particular sounds which either catch our attention or communicate something we want to know. All those who are not actually deaf can hear, but very few of us have developed the essential skills of listening that we increasingly need in a world in which the spoken word is rapidly becoming more important than the written. If we do not develop our listening skills, we fail to operate with full effectiveness as students, workers, managers, citizens, or anything else.

Without efficient listening skills we can never be sure that we have properly understood what we have heard. In many speaking situations people say things once only and if we miss them we have no opportunity to listen to them again. This is true of many lectures, meetings, speeches and broadcasts.

In lectures and many kinds of meetings we have to listen sufficiently well to remember, and recall when necessary, important things that others have said. This kind of listening, as we shall note, is closely associated with the activity of notemaking.

At a time when so much is being communicated to us by means of the spoken word, we have to discriminate and evaluate the relative significance and importance of a variety of utterances. Critical listening is an essential component of efficient listening.

Objectives

The basic objectives you should have (though you should, of course, add more specific objectives of your own to the list) are:

- Knowing the basic principles and requirements of efficient listening;
- Listening critically at all times;
- Listening with increasing efficiency in all interactive situations.

Methods

The listening activities we encounter we can group as follows:

- **Simple listening.** This category includes such everyday activities as telephone conversations, talking with friends and other conversational situations in which the listening is part of a more important social interaction rather than an activity in its own right. There is often little information of significance communicated in such situations.

- **Discriminative listening.** This term covers times when we try to separate sounds heard so that we do not listen to all the available sounds. Picking one sound out from others, as, for instance, in trying to identify one bird's singing among many or in trying to listen to what one person is saying at a noisy party or meeting, we could describe as discriminative listening.

- **Listening for relaxation**. Here the activity is very close to mere hearing because the act of relaxing is what is important and the listening – to conversation, stories, recordings, broadcasts and the like – is secondary. We listen in order to relax and have the mind and the attention diverted from everything else, rather than relax in order to listen.

- **Listening for information**. This is one of the main forms of the active, purposeful, systematic listening referred to earlier and we require it for assimilating announcements, listening to lectures, and so on. It is important here, as in the other kinds of listening which follow, to identify as clearly as possible what information you require from the source being listened to.

- **Listening to organise ideas**. In lectures, discussions, meetings and the like it is important to discriminate between one person's voice and another's and to listen effectively for information. In addition it is essential to organise one's thoughts and ideas about the information and to sort out mentally the relationships between various pieces of information and ideas expressed. We must assess the relative significance and importance of the various facts, ideas and opinions encountered, so that a coherent and meaningful mental picture emerges of what the lecture, discussion or meeting is about. Unless we can organise both our own thoughts and the expressed thoughts of others in this way, we are at a serious disadvantage in many social interaction situations.

- **Critical listening**. In many ways, critical listening is similar to critical reading and you should refer at this point to Chapter 7, page 67. Give particular attention when listening critically to both your own purposes in listening (for example, what do I need to know?) and to others' purposes in speaking (for example, what are they trying to tell me?). You should also pay attention to the problems of identifying bias, emotion, exaggeration, propaganda and the like in what other people say. In this way you are better equipped to reach an objective assessment.

- **Creative listening.** In listening to music, drama, films and similar aesthetic experiences, there is more involved than mere listening for pleasure or relaxation. You often require the ability to discriminate between sound patterns, as, for instance, in listening to music. The ability to assimilate the information contained in what you listen to is important, as is the ability to organise the facts, ideas, themes and so on into meaningful wholes. Above all, to obtain the greatest enjoyment and satisfaction, your critical faculties should respond to and appreciate the whole artistic creation in its total context. The more you know about a work, its creator, its predecessors, its philosophical or theoretical stimulus and its technique, the better your judgment and the more creatively fulfilling your listening.

The fourth, fifth and sixth kinds of listening described above will clearly interest people like students and managers. But if you are to fully develop your listening, you must practise all kinds of listening, rather than concentrating especially on those which appear to be directly relevant to your work or your studies. In this way, you obtain breadth as well as depth and you are better able to develop a flexible, systematic approach to listening.

We can outline seven methods of improving listening skills. Together they provide a basis for a systematic, efficient and developmental approach to listening:

1 *Notemaking.*
The efficient listener will always make notes where he or she can conveniently do this without inhibiting the person speaking. Memory is notoriously unreliable if untrained and, especially if you may have to refer later to what others have said, you may find a record of the content in note form invaluable. The notes should be as concise as possible and should concentrate on the main points. You should include necessary details within this framework. Aim to produce a short, coherent summary of the content of what someone has said. The act of preparing these notes will help to improve the quality of the listening itself in ways specified below.

2 *Defining purpose in listening.*
It is as important to know your purposes clearly when listening as

it is in any other activity. To help to define purposes you should decide:

- the nature of the material listened to (form and content, length, relevance, and so on);
- the reasons for listening to it (why you selected this particular material, how much information you require from it, how you will use the information, et cetera);
- expectations in listening (what you expect to hear and how this satisfies reasons for listening, how useful the information will be, how easy or difficult to understand, how interesting or dull, how entertaining or serious, and so on).

After listening, you should review the material and make some assessment of how far your purposes were satisfied and your expectations met. You should also consider how far defining purposes and expectations beforehand in this way improves the quality and efficiency of your listening.

3 *Active involvement in listening.*
Because listening is a receptive activity, like reading, it is easy to allow it to become passive. This leads to a loss of listening ability, with consequent effects on the ability to base effective decisions on what you have listened to. Active involvement is essential for efficient listening and most of the methods offered here for improving listening skills depend upon it for their success. Instead of simply sitting back and letting the information hit the ear drums, you should actively listen for the information that will satisfy your purposes and expectations as well as for information that you do not expect but which is relevant.

4 *Attentiveness.*
This is the basis of active involvement and an effective counter to passivity. You should give your whole attention, as far as possible, to whatever you listen to. Only in this way can you obtain a proper assimilation and understanding of the information presented. You should avoid distractions and use notemaking to help achieve this. You should avoid 'doodling' when making notes,

though it may indicate that what you are listening to does not command the attention sufficiently and may even not be worth listening to.

5 *Sensitivity.*
As a perceptive listener, you must be sensitive to many aspects of the material you listen to. It is not enough simply to be aware of the nature of the content, how it is organised and the purposes of the speaker as well as yourself. You must also be sensitive to:

- tone of voice (this can totally alter the significance of a statement);

- choice of words (many words have similar meanings, but the slight differences between them are critical);

- timing (when something is said is as important as how it is said);

- the speaker (there are many ways in which a speaker's personality can affect what is said and its significance – one person says something and, regardless of tone of voice, choice of words or anything else, people take it as a joke; another person says the same thing and offends people);

- the method of sound transmission (in the case of broadcasts or recordings where the nature of the means used to convey them enhances or impairs the meaning and significance – a speech will sound quite different when heard over a public address system outdoors from the way it will sound on a good quality tape recorder in a lounge);

- your own role in encouraging easy, fluent interaction (a listener can help speakers immensely by showing ar active interest in what they say and by smiling, nodding and agreeing at the appropriate points – see Chapter 11 on Body Language).

6 *Pattern of organisation.*
Except perhaps for long, rambling conversations of a personal, intimate nature, every discourse has a pattern of organisation. A

speaker wants to say something and he or she organises it into an acceptable form before beginning to speak. Otherwise, there might be a total failure to communicate with the audience. In the case of broadcasts, pieces of music and other recordings, the presence of pattern will be even more evident. The efficient listener must be able to identify the pattern imposed upon what he or she is listening to. It will often take this form:

- introduction (the subject or theme is briefly stated or outlined);

- development (the subject or theme is explored, discussed or explained in greater detail along the lines indicated in the introduction);

- conclusion (the conclusions drawn in the development are re-stated for emphasis or the audience is shown how the outline given in the introduction has been treated and given substance).

There are many variations which we can base on this simple pattern, but a listener should identify these three basic elements in most of the various kinds of material he or she encounters.

7 *Critical listening.*
Having listened to something, you should be able to say:

- what it was about;
- why it was said or presented;
- how it was organised; and
- how well it communicated (and, if it failed, how, where and why it failed).

Considering these aspects of what others communicate to us, as we saw in the chapter on reading, develops the ability to analyse critically. Here, it helps to improve listening skills further. The efficient listener should listen critically at all times.

Evaluation

Answer the following questions by selecting the most suitable option to complete each statement:

1 Skill in listening is important because:
  - *a) the spoken word is more difficult to understand than the written word*
  - *b) without it we should not really hear what people say to us*
  - *c) people tend to talk faster now than they used to*
  - *d) many things are said once only and if we miss them they are lost forever*

2 Efficient listening needs to be:
  - *a) active*
  - *b) passive*
  - *c) relaxed*
  - *d) time-consuming*

3 We should give particular attention, when listening critically, to:
  - *a) becoming as relaxed as possible*
  - *b) defining one's purposes in listening*
  - *c) avoiding all distractions*
  - *d) waiting until everything has been heard before analysing it*

4 If we are to fully develop listening skills:
  - *a) only those skills that are used should be trained*
  - *b) each skill should be developed in turn*
  - *c) there should be practice in all kinds of listening*
  - *d) a great deal of time has to be set aside for the purpose*

5 An activity which is especially helpful to efficient listening is:
  - *a) notemaking*
  - *b) summarising*
  - *c) memorising*
  - *d) thinking*

6 'Doodling' is:
  - *a) helpful to listening*
  - *b) a sign of wandering attention*

c) *part of notemaking*
d) *helpful to concentration*

7 One thing a perceptive listener must be sensitive to is:
a) *the time*
b) *the appearance of the speaker*
c) *the tone of voice*
d) *whether he or she agrees with what is being said*

8 A basic pattern of organisation for a speech is:
a) *conclusions, introduction, development*
b) *introduction, conclusions, summary*
c) *summary, introduction, conclusions*
d) *introduction, development, conclusion*

9 Critical listening should be carried out:
a) *systematically*
b) *quickly*
c) *cautiously*
d) *frequently*

10 After listening to something it should be:
a) *forgotten once notes have been made*
b) *reviewed and the content evaluated*
c) *listened to again whenever possible*
d) *summarised for future reference*

See page 189 for the answers to these questions.

Ongoing

You will find that your skill in listening will continue to improve if you carry out some of the following activities regularly:

- During the coming week, list the occasions on which you have used each of the seven kinds of listening described in this chapter. Which have you used most frequently? Which have you used least frequently? The following week, look for more opportunities to practise the kind of listening you used *least* frequently.

- Examine a day's radio programmes, as given in the *Radio Times*, and list the programmes under seven headings corresponding to the seven kinds of listening.

- Listen to a recording of a piece of music or a play and consider the relative importance to efficient listening of each of the seven kinds of listening. Repeat the exercise with a recording of a lecture or a discussion. What differences, and what similarities, in the kinds of listening required do you notice?

- Select a recording or short radio talk. Define your purposes in listening to it, along the lines suggested in this chapter, beforehand. As you listen to it, make notes that will satisfy your purposes in listening. Afterwards, compare your notes with your listed purposes. How far were your purposes satisfied?

- Listen to a short talk and note the significance and importance of the various aspects to which a listener needs to be sensitive (tone of voice, choice of words, timing, and so on).

- Listen to a talk and make notes. Afterwards, use these notes to prepare a plan of the pattern of organisation of the material.

- Listen to a recording made while several people are talking at once. How easy or difficult is it to listen to one person in particular?

- Listen to a recording of a discussion or a meeting and then write a coherent and logically ordered statement of the points dealt with and the matters discussed.

Completion checklist

At the end of this chapter you should be able to answer the following questions:

1 How many of the seven kinds of listening can you list?
2 How many of the seven methods of improving listening skills can you list?
3 What form will the pattern of organisation of a discourse often take?

4 How does listening, as defined here, differ from hearing?
5 What is critical listening similar to?
6 To help define purpose in listening, what should you decide?
7 How is listening similar to reading?

Conclusion

It is easier to develop listening skills if you are a member of a group that is trying to find ways of improving. This is also true of presentation skills. But you can achieve a great deal on your own if you follow the advice and guidance given in this chapter and if you will find some time to try out some of the Ongoing exercises.

Motivation and practice can overcome many obstacles along the road to self-improvement, no matter what skill you wish to develop.

Review what you have learned from this chapter before you go to sleep tonight.

9

EFFECTIVE WRITING

Of all the skills covered in this book, writing is probably alone in that we do receive a certain amount of continuing instruction in writing techniques when we make our way through the educational process. Unfortunately, very often the kinds of writing in which we receive the most practice – essays, compositions, stories and personal letters – are not the kinds of writing we have to do when we begin working for our living. Indeed, they are frequently the kinds of writing least required of us.

Teachers mark our work for us and we receive high marks or low according to their subjective assessment of our abilities. They do not teach us any objective methods which enable us to make some self-assessment of our writing. Yet such methods exist and they can be of some use to us if we use them wisely and with care.

Teachers do not show us how to use a systematic strategy when approaching writing tasks and consequently we tend to work in very amateurish and ineffective ways. We lack a method for collecting information together in such a way that it is then easier to construct a pattern of organisation that will make our material more attractive and easier to read. They very rarely give us sound practical hints and tips on how to make writing more readable and hence more effective. They do not even introduce many of us to, let alone train us to understand, some of the basic technical language of grammar, so that we are aware of the nature, cause and possible remedy for many of the errors we commit. It is not at all rare to find people educated since the Second World War – and that covers a great many people – who do not know what a noun or verb or adjective is, let alone a clause or a gerund (if any of these terms are new to you, you should look them up in a grammar handbook).

We are not taught how to edit and polish our writing so that it makes the most favourable impression possible upon the reader. We are not told about the various factors which can improve or impede legibility and readability. Nor do we pay much attention to layout, although this is a crucial factor in gaining or losing the reader's attention even before he or she has begun reading.

Here we shall concentrate on what is of practical value to people who find they have difficulties with the reports, memos, letters and other materials which they have to produce in the course of their work. In doing this, we shall look at some of the approaches and techniques often used by professional writers. After all, many of you will be professionals in various fields. Why then should you have to become amateurs when you write, simply through a lack of knowledge of a professional writing approach?

Review

Before you read any further, carry out the following exercise. You will gain the greatest benefit from it if you do not look ahead. Make sure you have some paper and a pen or pencil to hand and that you have no interruptions.

You have 20 minutes in which to write a short report on one of the following topics:

1 The duties of your post (as if for a new superior);

2 Your achievements at work in the past 12 months, 6 months or month (or other convenient period of time);

3 Your plans at work for the next 12 months, 6 months or month (or other convenient period of time);

4 The contribution your organisation makes to the local, regional or national economy;

5 An accident at work;

6 Your organisation is to take a stand at a trade exhibition and you have to report on the contribution your department or section could make;

7 Your organisation considers relocating to another part of the country and you have to report on the advantages and disadvantages;

8 Report on a visit to one of your organisation's other factories, offices or sites;

9 Report on your subordinates at work (as if for a performance appraisal);

10 Report on how you would eliminate unemployment (assuming only democratic powers).

Alternatively, you may write any kind of report on any subject of your own choice. The objective is to produce 100–200 words which will then be subject to analysis. You will be shown how to do this for yourself.

It is important that you should write the text of the report in sentences and paragraphs. One of the methods of analysis which we shall use will not work with lists of points that are not sentences, or are tables of figures or visual ways of presenting information that you might use in reports. Other than that, do whatever you would do in producing a report in terms of the organisation and layout.

Remember you have no more than 20 minutes. As soon as you are ready, you can begin. Do not read on until you have finished.

Exercise review

We shall carry out the analysis in two parts: qualitative and quantitative.

First of all, then, the qualitative aspects of your writing.

- Did you plan what you were going to do before you began writing? Even with a short exercise like this, a minute or so spent planning is time well spent. The worst way to tackle any writing task is just to begin writing without any idea of where you are going and the points you are going to make.
- Does the report have a title? All reports should have titles.
- Is the report prefaced by a brief summary? Even with a short piece like the one you have just written, a brief summary, abstract or synopsis of the main points is useful both to the

reader in a hurry and the reader who is going to read the whole report anyway.

- Have you given the sections of the report any necessary headings and (if required) sub-headings? One of the things that differentiates reports from other kinds of writing is that each section has a heading.
- If you have used headings, have you used a system of identifying those headings? The most commonly used method these days is the decimal system (i.e., 1, 1.1, 1.1.1).

Now, on the quantitative side, carry out the following steps. You will find this easier if you have a calculator available.

1 Count the number of words you have written (excluding the title and headings if used);
2 Count the number of sentences;
3 Count the number of polysyllabic (long) words (i.e., words which have more than two syllables or sound segments) – if you find this difficult, count the number of words which have seven letters or more. If you wish to be precise about this, you should exclude from the count all proper nouns, combinations of short, simpler words like troubleshooting, roundabout, countryside, undertaking, overlooking and caretaker, and words where the third syllable is -es, or -ed, like services or expected;
4 Calculate the average sentence length (the number of words divided by the number of sentences);
5 Calculate the percentage of polysyllabic words (or words with seven letters or more). If you find this difficult, you may find it easier to count the number of long words in the first 100 words, as a number per hundred is, of course, automatically a percentage. This short-cut figure will serve our purposes here.

Your average sentence length should be less than 20 words and the percentage of polysyllabic words should be less than 10 per cent. If either figure is higher than this, your readers could have a problem and, if they have a problem, *you* have a problem. You are writing for your readers, after all, not for yourself.

You can use the two pieces of information you have (average sentence length and percentage of long words) to calculate what is known as the *Fog Index*, or an index of how likely your writing is to be clear or lacking in clarity (foggy). The calculation is:

0.4 (*average sentence length* + % *polysyllables*)

For example, if average sentence length = 20 and % polysyllables = 10, then:

$$0.4\ (20 + 10) = 12$$

The figure you finish up with, according to the research into readability, roughly equates to the number of years of full-time education someone will need to have had in order to read, with reasonable ease and efficiency, what you have written. So figures higher than about 11 mean you are writing for people who stayed on at school, since most people these days receive at least 11 years of compulsory education. Higher figures mean you are writing for people who went to university and figures higher than about 16 mean you are writing for a post-graduate readership.

This is, of course, a very simple and crude measure, but it does have its uses. Any piece of writing where the Fog Index is higher than 16 should be examined closely. See if you can split any of the long sentences and replace any of the long words by shorter ones without affecting the meaning.

Problems

The most common problems we encounter in writing are as follows:

- Failure to check the accuracy of what is written;
- Failure to control the length of what is written;
- The meaning is not always clear;
- Paying little attention to keeping writing as simple as possible;
- Lack of a clear sense of purpose in writing;

- Inability to suit the order and arrangement to the purpose in writing and the nature of the material to ensure effectiveness;

- Carrying out preparatory work haphazardly and not working to a plan;

- Inability to change the style of writing to suit different purposes or materials;

- Writing contains many common structural and grammatical errors;

- You write only when you cannot avoid it;

- Limited vocabulary;

- Spelling difficulties;

- Punctuation difficulties;

- Writing has no identifiable style and is not easy to read rapidly and efficiently;

- Illegible writing;

- Limited general background of knowledge and experience.

Objectives

The basic objectives you should have (though you should, of course, add more specific objectives of your own to the list) are:

- Using an effective strategy for writing;
- Knowing how to plan before writing;
- Following the principles and techniques of effective writing;
- Knowing how to analyse your writing;
- Understanding the need for 'incubation' periods when writing.

Methods

When you write something, whether it is a report, a letter, a memo, an autobiography or even a novel, you need to progress through four main stages.

1 You have to collect your information or ideas – your material – together before you can organise it.
2 You have to organise it before you can write it.
3 You have to write it before you can edit and polish it.
4 You have to edit and polish it to ensure that it is in the best possible state for presentation to the reader.

The writing strategy outlined in this section is, quite simply, based on these four stages, with the addition of another important element – the incubation period. The nature and value of this will be explained shortly.

An effective writing strategy consists, then, of five stages: *Preparation, Assessment, Planning, Expression and Review.* Taking the initial letters of each stage, we have the **PAPER** strategy for effective writing. Let us look at each of these in more detail and see what steps have to be taken within each stage.

First of all, let us consider *Preparation.* The first step in this stage is to make sure you are clear about your terms of reference. In other words, you need to know as much as you can about the scope of the report, memo, letter or whatever it is that you are writing. What topics will you cover and in what depth? Who will read it? Why are you writing it? When does it have to be finished by? Where is it to go? How is it to be produced (that is, what resources do you have at your disposal in the way of financial, secretarial or other help, or technical equipment)?

Next, you need to focus more closely on the readership and ask some more questions. *Who*, exactly, is the piece of writing for? What do you know about them? How much do they know about the subject already? Do they have any known attitudes or opinions which may need to be taken into account? What do they need to know (there is not much point in telling the reader things he or she knows already, nor is there much point in conveying information simply because you have happened to discover it)? Are there any special considerations you have to bear in mind, such as that the reader is a non-technical person and this is a technical subject? What response or reaction do you require from the reader? What kind of relationship do you wish to establish with the reader (will you address him or her as 'you' and yourself as 'I' or 'we' or will you use the third person singular past tense passive voice of much scientific writing – 'It was discovered that . . .')? What assumptions about the subject will the readers have made and what assumptions have you made? You may, of course, ask other questions, but you should at least have clear answers for these.

Now you need to focus more closely on *why* you are writing the piece. What are the objectives you are seeking to achieve? It is worth writing these down, beginning with the words: 'The report/letter/memo/etc. will . . .' Will what? The more precise you are about what you intend to do, the more likely you are to succeed. Remember in doing this that objectives are like targets and goals and you should express them accurately and in the form of results to achieve. Aims, intentions and purposes are usually rather more vague and less quantifiable, therefore they are less useful in helping us to know later whether or not we achieved what we set out to do.

Once you have a clear picture of your terms of reference, your readership and your objectives, you are then in a position to collect your information and ideas together in a more meaningful and useful way. You also need to have some means of storing the information you gather so that you can easily gain access to it later.

In making notes, it is useful to use two techniques: self-recitation and mind-mapping. For those readers who have not yet worked through earlier chapters and to remind those who have, self-recitation means asking six simple questions:

What?
Why?
When?
How?
Where?
Who?

Mind-mapping simply means that instead of making notes as a list of points, you make them by radiating out from a central topic point. These two techniques in combination offer a free-flowing, flexible and effective method of drawing information and ideas together without becoming tied to a particular pattern of organisation at too early a stage of the writing process. Lists tend to become fixed and we believe that the things we think of, and write down, first are the most important, which might not necessarily be the case. Once all the information and ideas are to hand you can then move on to the next stage, *Assessment*.

In the Assessment stage, you simply set aside some time during which you can detach yourself from what you have done so far, think about other things for a while and then return to your work with a degree of objectivity. This is necessary if you are to spot errors, defects and deficiencies in what you have done. To try to assess the quality of your work without an incubation period of this kind is to risk missing faults simply because you are too involved with the material, too close to it and therefore likely to overlook mistakes. The best kind of incubation period is the overnight break and you will certainly need one of these between the Expression and Review stages if at all possible. But you can use life's other little natural breaks as incubation periods – lunchbreaks, teabreaks, telephone calls – any change of activity which will enable you to return to your work with a degree of objectivity and therefore a more critical eye.

Once you have checked the completeness of your preparation and ensured that you are in every way ready to proceed, you can move on to *Planning*. Here you have to make the final decision on the form of the report, letter, memo or whatever it is you are writing. If you change your mind after this point, you will need to do some re-working and you should avoid this if at all possible. You must now select and organise your information. You have to identify a logical sequence and decide how many sections or paragraphs to break the material down into. If it is a report, you have to identify headings which will describe quickly and accurately the contents of each section and you have to put the sections in a logical order. An example of a plan, based upon the PAPER strategy for writing reports is given in Figure 9.1 overleaf.

Once you have a good, detailed plan, you need another Assessment stage or incubation period. It is important to get the plan right. If you do, what follows will virtually write itself and there will be much less chance of mistakes being made in grammar, spelling and punctuation. Errors in these areas are more common if the material as a whole is disorganised and lacking in coherence. A good motto to keep in mind is the **5P Principle: Proper planning prevents poor performance.**

Figure 9.1

The PAPER Strategy

1. PREPARATION	Clarify terms of reference Analyse readership Set objectives Collect information Store information
2. ASSESSMENT	Set aside time for an incubation period Check completeness of preparation Ensure readiness to proceed
3. PLANNING	Make final decision on form of communication Select information Plan arrangement of information selected Organise body, using appropriate headings Complete all pre-expression stages Allow for an incubation period where possible
4. EXPRESSION	Write a first draft Complete the writing within as short a period of time as possible Write body first, then introduction, then any other parts and write summary/abstract/synopsis last Follow the principles and techniques of effective writing Keep expression as short as possible Use short paragraphs, but vary structure Use short sentences, but vary structure Use illustrative material whenever appropriate Keep the reader in mind *all* the time Allow for an incubation period where possible
5. REVIEW	Carry out a detailed analysis Assess readability Edit, add, amend, delete as necessary Assess readability again Determine layout Allow for an incubation period where possible Check again Be sure you are satisfied with the final version If there is time, check yet again Send or submit

If the incubation period shows, on return to the material, that you need no further changes to the plan, you can move on to the next stage, *Expression*. Many professional writers, at this point, will write a first draft. They will not try to achieve perfection immediately. Trying to get each sentence and each paragraph just right as you go along is a very slow and inefficient method of working. The problem is that, whatever difficulties there are in saying exactly what you want to say, you are trying to do so with an inevitably incomplete awareness of the total context in which you make any changes. This is because, at any point, part of what you want to say is written down, but the rest is still in your head and it is virtually impossible, therefore, to predict the consequence of any changes upon the document as a whole.

Write the report, letter, memo or whatever it is at a single sitting wherever possible. The shorter the period of time over which you write the first draft, the better the chance that you will finish with the same concept in your mind of your initial aims and objectives. Conversely, the longer the period over which you do the writing, the greater the danger that you will, perhaps slightly but significantly, change your idea of what you want to achieve and, hence, your way of doing and saying it. If the document is simply too long to be completed at a single sitting, try to end each writing session at the end of a section. Give yourself the first sentence of the next section, if you like, as your starter, but try not to leave things in the middle. If you do, you will nearly always have to go back over much of your already written material to get yourself into the same frame of mind that you were in previously. This is not only wasteful of time, but it is also highly likely to produce problems in expressing yourself which you can easily avoid by working in the way suggested here.

Write the body of the text first, then the introduction, then any remaining parts of the document, leaving the summary or abstract or synopsis, if there is one, till last. The reason for this is that it is much easier to write an introduction when you can see clearly what it is you are introducing. It is also much easier to write a summary which truly highlights the key points when you have the whole thing in front of you.

As you write, follow the principles and techniques of effective writing. The main ones you should bear in mind are:

- Keep the expression as short as possible. There is no virtue in making things longer than necessary.

- Use short paragraphs, but vary the structure. Only use single sentence paragraphs to emphasise particularly important points. As a reasonable rule of thumb, paragraphs should be between about five and ten lines in length. Longer than ten lines can be intimidating for many readers.
- Use short sentences, but vary the structure. Variety is, after all, the spice of life and, in itself, helps to make material more interesting (or, at least, less uninteresting).
- Use short words rather than long ones whenever it is appropriate.
- Use illustrative material whenever it will help to make a point more effectively. They do say a picture is worth a thousand words.
- Use direct statement with active verbs in preference to the passive voice. Better to say 'We discovered . . .' rather than 'It was discovered that . . .'. Research shows that passive (and negative) statements require much more work by the brain than active (and positive) statements. Readers are therefore much more likely to misunderstand them.
- Omit qualifying phrases unless they are essential to the sense of sentences.
- Preserve the unity of each sentence and each paragraph. In other words, each sentence should have one subject and each paragraph should deal with a single topic.
- Make sure you know the meanings of the words you use. Do not use a new word you are not sure of just to try to impress.
- Above all, keep the readers in mind and write for them. Rather than ask yourself: How can I say this? ask: How will the readers best understand this? This will tend to draw the right words out. It is, after all, always easier to solve someone else's problems than your own.

Once the first draft is complete, it is desirable to allow for another incubation period. This is the one which, you may recall, should preferably be at least an overnight break. In this way you have a better chance of returning to edit your material with a genuine and useful degree of objectivity. You can then look at your writing almost as if someone else had written it.

The first step in the *Review* stage is to carry out a detailed analysis of your writing. You should do this in two parts. First of all, you should check that the document says what you wanted it to say, in other words, a check on the meaning. Secondly, you should check the mechanics and technicalities of organisation and expression to ensure that there are no grammatical, punctuation, spelling or other errors. The reason for having two checks is that it is very difficult to check for both sets of possible errors at one and the same time. The best way is to have two people checking. The one who has written the material can read it aloud and another person can follow the text on paper.

Some useful questions to ask as you check are:

On the meaning:

1 Are there any unnecessary repetitions?
2 Is there any ambiguity?
3 Have you kept your readers in mind and written for them?
4 Are there any contradictions?
5 Are facts clearly differentiated from opinions?
6 Are all conclusions and recommendations (if present) clearly justified by the facts given?
7 Can you read the summary (if there is one) and understand it without referring to the rest of the document?
8 If you received the document, would you know how to respond to it?
9 Is any of the information more suitable for presentation as a diagram or graph or other visual form?
10 Have you checked the readability by calculating the Fog Index (on a long document, you need only do it for a sample of the material)?

On the structure:

1 Is each section in its proper place?
2 Is any section badly planned?
3 Are there any parts where material should be taken out and placed in an appendix?
4 Have the punctuation and spelling been checked?
5 Is the layout attractive?
6 Have you written with grammatical correctness?
7 Are you satisfied with your paragraph and sentence structure?
8 If the material is typewritten, are there any typographical errors?
9 Would a table of contents help the readers to find things?
10 Are you completely satisfied with the document? If you have time, check it again or ask someone else to check it.

Once a detailed analysis has been carried out, you should check the readability, if you have not already done so, using the method you used at the beginning of this chapter. Edit, add, amend, delete as necessary to bring the readability up to an appropriate level and to remove any errors revealed by asking the questions above. If you have made many changes, you may need to assess the readability again.

Decide upon the layout, remembering to allow plenty of space. There is no point in cramming as much as you can into as small a space as possible. That will not help the reader. Allow for another incubation period at this point, if time allows. Check everything again. Make sure you are satisfied with the final version. If there is time, check yet again. In other words, it is like the old advice given to students taking examinations: Never leave early. If you finish early, use the time to check. You might just find that little mistake which will make all the difference between a credit and a distinction – or a pass and a fail depending where you are on life's little ladder. When you have done all you reasonably can to correct and polish your document, send or submit it to the intended readers. You have at least done your best for them.

There is clearly a great deal more which we could say about effective writing, but, hopefully, we have covered the essentials and provided you with some tools and techniques which you can begin to use straightaway to improve the quality and effectiveness of your own writing. If you put the guidance given here into effect and carry out the activities described in the Ongoing section, you should find, gradually, that writing becomes less of a chore, even if it never becomes a positive pleasure. Some readers, though, will find that they do begin to actually enjoy writing and get satisfaction out of the exercise of their developing skills.

Evaluation

Apply the practical advice given in this chapter to the following paragraph in order to improve its readability and overall effectiveness:

> A report is an ordered and logical statement, with appropriate use of sectional headings and sub-headings, of the facts about a situation or problem, the case for and/or against a proposed course of action, a description and evaluation of the results of

work or research, or a record of a sequence of events, with interpretation of the significance of specific events within the sequence, together with any necessary resultant conclusions and/or recommendations, and any supporting evidence, illustrative materials, or other appendices. Normally, the report will be prefaced by a brief summary.

As it stands, that paragraph has a Fog Index of 26.6.

For an alternative version, against which to compare your own, see the Answers section on page 190.

Ongoing

You will find that your skill in writing will continue to improve if you carry out some of the following activities regularly:

- Keep a diary of the kind that will require you to write a few lines at least about the events of each day.
- Write at least one letter a week to someone you know you ought to keep in touch with but never seem to have the time to. Make time.
- Write a letter to a newspaper on an issue about which you feel strongly. There is something very satisfying about seeing your name in print. Some papers even pay for letters.
- Write an article for a journal on a subject about which you consider yourself something of an expert.
- Write a report about yourself and your career. Where are you? How did you get there? Where do you see yourself going?
- Write your autobiography or the story of your family within your own (and others') living memory as if for your children or grandchildren yet unborn.
- Keep a detailed diary of your next trip abroad whether for business or pleasure.
- Make a list of all the things you think are wrong with a public service like the railways, the Post Office or the telephone service and then write a letter to the respective customer services department.
- Write a short story.
- Go for the big one – write a novel.

Completion checklist

At the end of this chapter you should be able to answer the following questions:

1 What is the Fog Index?
2 How many of the most common problems we encounter in writing can you list?
3 What are the five steps in the PAPER strategy?
4 What is the best kind of incubation period?
5 Why is it best to write something over as short a period of time as possible?
6 In what order should the parts of a document be written?
7 How many of the principles and techniques of effective writing can you list?
8 How many of the questions you should use when checking can you list?

Conclusion

We shall not have solved all your problems in writing with the contents of this short chapter, but, with a little luck, we may have started a process which can now continue for the rest of your life. You can continue improving for as long as you keep trying to put the guidance given here into practice.

If, in the process, writing becomes a more manageable and more effective activity in which progressively less time is taken to complete writing tasks, by working systematically using the PAPER strategy, you will have made a useful achievement.

Review what you have learned from this chapter before you go to sleep tonight.

10

PRESENTATION SKILLS

The importance of being able to stand up (or even sit) in front of a group of people and make a presentation of a proposal or give a speech or lead a discussion of some kind is yet another neglected skill. Some people do develop these skills to some extent by being active in school debating societies or school plays, but most of us leave school never having had to prepare, plan and deliver a speech of any kind to our peers. Incidentally, when the word 'presentation' is used here, you can take it to refer to any situation in which one or more persons are presenting information (or reflections or ideas) to a group of other people.

These skills, however, are not difficult to learn. With practice, confidence develops and with growing confidence, greater skill. We can even use a variation of the strategy we encountered in the last chapter. In this way, we can overcome what for most people is the greatest deterrent to standing up and speaking out in public – the fear that they will make fools of themselves. By working with the familiar and by being systematic in our approach again, we shall give ourselves the necessary degree of confidence to ensure that such an outcome is a remote possibility.

Review

For this chapter, you will need a tape recorder if you are to derive the maximum benefit from it. If you have access to video-taping facilities, this will be even better as you will be able to see as well as hear yourself. If you are able to video-tape yourself when carrying out the exercises in this chapter, save the tape because you may find it useful in relation to Chapter 11 on Body Language.

For this first exercise, have your recording equipment ready and a watch or some other timing device. Find a place where you will not be disturbed for a few minutes and where you will not be overheard.

When you are ready, start recording and speak for one minute on any topic of your choice. For those who find it difficult to think of a topic on the spur of the moment, here are some suggestions:

- Your hobby.
- Your favourite TV programme.
- Your job.
- Your last holiday.
- A topic currently in the news about which you feel strongly.
- Your car and its various facilities and equipment.
- Your family.
- Your future ambitions.
- Your achievements so far in life.
- What the government should be doing to improve society.

When you have finished, play the tape back and then ask yourself the following questions:

1 Did you decide on the precise limits of the topic before you began speaking?
2 Who did you have in mind as an audience?
3 Did you give yourself a purpose for the talk?
4 Did you structure what you were going to say beforehand?
5 Did your voice come over loud and clear?
6 Were there many 'ums' and 'ers'?
7 Were there any pauses that were too long?
8 Were there any places where a pause would have let a point sink in?

9 Did you feel nervous?
10 Overall, were you reasonably pleased with the result?

At this stage, you may well find that you simply started talking without giving much thought to what, how and why you were speaking and who you were addressing. As we shall see, these are factors which are important if we are to speak effectively whatever the situation.

Problems

- **Nervousness** is probably the most common problem experienced by most people in any public speaking context. In some cases this can be so bad that it amounts to outright fear. You should not worry too much about being nervous because most people are at least a little nervous when they are the centre of attention. Indeed, many actors say that a little nervousness is desirable because it keeps you on your toes and helps to ensure that you give of your best. In any event, no matter how nervous you feel, it is unlikely that it will show to your audience. You might feel that it is obvious that you are nervous, but an audience will be concentrating more on what you have to say than on whether you appear nervous or not.

- **Failure to define the audience clearly** is another fault. Some people become so wrapped up in their own problems of putting what they want to say into words that they forget that different listeners will have different needs. There are few things more irritating than listening to a speaker who is so oblivious of the audience that it would not really matter whether or not they were there at all.
- **Failure to define the precise limits of the topic** often accompanies failure to define the audience. The speaker rambles on with no regard for the audience's interest in the topic and willingness to listen.
- **Lack of purpose** causes problems for both speaker and listeners. Quite simply, if a speaker has no clear sense of purpose in speaking this will make it almost impossible for the audience to tell exactly what kinds of things they should be listening for. Everybody becomes confused.

- **Lack of structure** means that what is said has no recognisable shape; no clear beginning, middle and end. This also makes it difficult for the audience to decide what they should be listening for. It also means that the speaker is much more likely to meander around the subject, repeating things that have already been said and often missing out altogether key elements that would be of interest to listeners.
- **Delivery** is a problem for most inexperienced speakers. They talk too loudly or too softly, they pause in the wrong places and for too long (another consequence of lack of preparation and planning), they 'um' and 'er' too much and make other speech errors. You will need to listen to yourself very carefully to decide whether or not you are guilty of any of these faults. If you can practise speaking in front of a sympathetic listener, they should be able to tell you whether or not you need to make any changes in your delivery. However, even if there is no one readily available, you should be able to use the advice given in this chapter to help you to make your own mind up.

Objectives

The basic objectives you should have (though you should, of course, add more specific objectives of your own to the list) are:

- Knowing how to collect together material for a presentation;
- Knowing how to plan a presentation;
- Delivering a presentation with greater confidence and skill;
- Reviewing your performance in a presentation to identify ways of improving future presentations.

Methods

A variation of the PAPER strategy will serve us well in our quest to improve our presentation skills, whether we are making a formal presentation to a large number of people or simply an informal one to a group of colleagues at work. Indeed, the PAPER strategy can, with appropriate modifications, be used to help us to improve our effectiveness generally in communicating with others whether by means of the spoken or the written word or any other medium of expression. This is because it is based around the four principal activities that must be included in any successful communication:

- collecting information
- structuring information
- expressing information
- reviewing the result.

Preparation, then, is the first stage. You must be clear in your own mind what the scope of your presentation is to be. How much information are you going to give your listeners? How much do they need? In other words, what are your terms of reference? What do you know about your audience? How much can you find out about them? The more closely you know them, the more precisely you can target your presentation, speech, talk, lecture or leading of the discussion to meet their needs.

Make sure you have clear objectives in mind that you are seeking to achieve and remember that these should be expressed as results to be achieved. It is always worth writing your objectives down for future reference. Once you have clear terms of reference, a clear picture of the audience and clear objectives, then you can collect together the information on which your presentation will be based and store it in a convenient form. Refer to page 80 for more on notemaking and storing information. To put all this as simply as possible, you must know what you are talking about.

Once all the Preparation has been done, an *Assessment* period will enable you to go away and then return and look at what you have done up to this point with a degree of objectivity. Check the completeness of your preparation and ensure that you are ready to proceed.

As in writing, *Planning* is the key stage in getting ready for a presentation. Make the final decision on the form of the presentation, covering such things as the length, whether it is to be formal or informal and whether you will make it standing up or sitting down (generally speaking, only informal presentations to small groups of people should be made sitting down as your presentation will have more impact if you make it standing up). Select the information you will present to your audience and structure it in a logical sequence. Do not try to tell them too much. It is better to get half a dozen points firmly home than to reel off masses of facts which don't even touch the sides as they pass through the audience's ears.

There are at least three basic patterns for presentations. Most of the time it will be easiest to structure them in three parts:

- Introduction – tell them what you are going to tell them.
- Body – tell them.
- Conclusion – tell them what you have told them.

On other occasions, it may be more appropriate to use a journey format. This is common for training-style presentations:

- Where are we? The situation at present.
- Where do we want to go? The objective.
- How will we get there? The methods to be used.
- How will we know we have arrived? Evaluation of performance.
- Where do we go next? Continuation and follow-up procedures.

A third method is to use the journalist's questions (or Kipling's 'serving men'), which, for those who have not encountered them yet in earlier chapters, are:

What?
Why?
When?
How?
Where?
Who?

You use whichever questions fit the nature of your presentation and put them in the order which best suits the subject.

Make notes to assist you in case you 'dry up' and make sure these notes are written in letters large enough to see when you are standing and they are resting, say, on a table in front of you. Make the notes on cards. These rattle less than sheets of A4 paper if you happen to be nervous. Number the cards clearly and link them together by punching a hole in the top left hand corner and running a treasury tag through it. Any good stationer will know what treasury tags are if you are unfamiliar with the term.

Until you have developed some skill in making presentations, it is a good idea to write out the presentation in full first and make your notes from this. It is also a good idea to learn the Introduction and the Conclusion off by heart. Then at least you will not be lost for words at the beginning of your talk and you will also be able to devise a good, strong ending for it. Have your full version with you as extra insurance. Then, at the very worst, you can read it out and still salvage something from the occasion. You will almost certainly find, however, that just knowing you have the full version if you need it will mean that you won't. It is an effective method of boosting confidence.

Once the presentation is planned, another incubation or assessment period is useful. If you plan well in advance of the occasion, it should not be difficult to programme the necessary time for this into the process.

When it comes to the *Expression* stage, or the actual making of the presentation, there are several standard pieces of advice which can be given. It might be helpful if you have a checklist to refer to:

- Rehearse at least once beforehand.
- Keep it as short as you can without missing anything important out.
- Speak with the aid of notes.
- Speak naturally and loud enough so that all your audience can hear clearly.
- Establish eye contact with as many members of your audience as possible.
- Avoid mannerisms, poses and too much walking about.
- Use examples your audience will understand to illustrate your points.
- Use statistics very sparingly and carefully.
- Speak *to* your audience rather than *at* them.
- Use illustrative material and visual aids whenever appropriate.
- Keep the listener in mind all the time.

- Have a glass of water to hand in case your mouth feels dry.

- Don't rush through your presentation. Allow reasonable pauses to let important points sink in.

- Avoid or at least explain jargon if you must use it.

- Use handouts if you have a lot of detail to communicate.

- Only use humour if it comes naturally to you. There is nothing worse than a forced joke told by someone who is not very good at it.

- Vary the tone, pitch, volume and speed of speaking a little to make things sound more interesting and lively.

- Keep your hands out of your pockets (if you have pockets) and don't fold your arms across your chest. Both are often perceived as negative or defensive postures.

- Try to avoid speech errors (but not completely, as speech without any errors may be perceived as glib).

- Relax. Remember that everyone finds making presentations stressful. If you have followed all the other advice given here, your audience will in any case be willing you to succeed.

Wherever it can be done without intruding into the occasion, it is useful to tape presentations for subsequent review and analysis. Video is better, but sound only will still enable you to tell a number of things about how the presentation went. This *Review* stage is important in enabling you to learn from the experience and take action to produce an improved performance on the next occasion.

Some questions you might ask yourself are:

1 Did you achieve your objectives?
2 If you failed in any way, how, whereabouts and why did you fail?
3 How could you have improved upon your delivery?
4 How could you have improved upon your content?
5 How could you have improved upon your visual aids?
6 What other lessons can be learned from this experience?

Evaluation

Using the guidance and advice given in this chapter, prepare a five minute presentation on a topic of your own choice. Make it. Record it. Analyse it afterwards. Compare it with the brief presentation you made at the beginning of the chapter. What differences do you notice? Are these differences improvements? Do you feel that you have improved? Do you notice any new elements of your style and approach which could be improved upon? Are you still guilty of any faults you thought you had eradicated?

Ongoing

You will find that your skill in making presentations of all kinds will continue to improve if you carry out some of the following activities regularly:

- Prepare a short 5-minute presentation (though you can try longer ones if you wish) every month for recording and analysis.
- Analyse other people's presentations in the way you analyse your own to see what can be learned from them.
- Every week speak for one minute on a topic in the news. Record and analyse.
- Actively seek chances to contribute to the discussion at any meetings you attend whether at work or outside.
- Find out what visual aids for presentations are available at work and ask someone who knows to show you how to use them. What are their relative advantages and disadvantages?

Completion checklist

At the end of this chapter you should be able to answer the following questions:

1 What is probably the most common problem experienced by most people in public speaking?
2 For whom does lack of purpose in speaking cause problems?
3 Give two of the reasons stated why delivery is a problem for most inexperienced speakers.
4 Name the five stages of the PAPER strategy.

5 Describe two of the basic patterns for presentations.
6 What is it a good idea to do until you have developed some skill in making presentations?
7 What questions should you ask when you review a presentation?

Conclusion

Making presentations can be a nerve-wracking experience or it can be fun. A lot depends upon your attitude towards them and how systematically you prepare and, particularly, plan what you are going to do in advance. If you follow the advice and guidance offered here, you should certainly find them less stressful in future and you should have a good chance of finding them rewarding and satisfying. You are, after all, in a position to influence the thinking and actions of others and that is quite an achievement.

Review what you have learned from this chapter before you go to sleep tonight.

11

BODY LANGUAGE

Most of us are managers of one kind or another. We may be chief executives of multinational corporations; we may be managers of small shops with only one or two part-time staff or we may be managers of a family. If we are not managers, then we are certainly customers, clients, colleagues or friends. In other words, whatever our role in life, we have to deal with people. We have to communicate with them.

Life is a communication-centred activity. If we cannot communicate effectively, we cannot live effectively.

Most of us assume that, because whatever teaching we have had in communication skills has been primarily verbal, verbal communication must be the most important form of communication. This is not necessarily the case. One American researcher claims that up to 93 per cent of the impact in a face-to-face message is, in fact, nonverbal. In other words, body language is more powerful than speech. Indeed, another researcher has discovered that if body language and spoken language conflict, it is the body language that is believed. So an understanding and mastery of body language is vital to everybody who deals with people in the course of their working or leisure day. That means all of us, unless you live as a hermit in a cave somewhere.

We all have a great deal of intuitive awareness, knowledge and expertise in using body language. After all, we have been using it all our lives. In many cases, research has done no more than confirm the obvious, but in others the findings are surprising and, with training, useful.

Review

Consider these questions and write down brief answers to them:

1 Why don't people look at each other in lifts and on the tube?
2 Why don't people smile as they walk to work in the morning?
3 Why do people nod when listening to someone else?
4 Why do so many people fold their arms or put their hands in their pockets when making a presentation?
5 Why do people lean forward when they are interested?
6 What is a comfortable distance between two people when they are standing talking?
7 Why do so many people not like being touched by other people?
8 What can you tell about a person from the way they dress?
9 Why do some people 'talk across' other people in a discussion?
10 How would you use your voice to encourage someone to trust you?

As you read the chapter which follows, look particularly for statements which conflict with the answers you have given. They may help you to learn something very useful to you specifically as an individual. This does not mean that you have to agree with everything that is said here, but do bear in mind that all the guidance and advice given is based on research into body language (or nonverbal communication as psychologists, anthropologists, sociologists and other students of human and animal behaviour prefer to call it).

Problems

One of the main reasons that many people experience problems in using body language effectively is that their education has emphasised verbal communication and neglected the nonverbal aspect. As we have seen before in considering the topics covered in other chapters, there are many skills which schools, colleges and universities neglect. This is one of the most important ones, for, although we have been 'speaking' body language from birth, the absence of any training in how to use it more effectively means our skills are not as developed as they might be.

Context is a major problem in using body language to better effect. There are very few movements or gestures that have a universal meaning, regardless of the culture in which they occur. You cannot take a particular posture or bodily movement and say that it always means the same thing whenever it occurs. You cannot say that every time a person scratches his or her nose he or she is trying to deceive someone. It is an indication that something may be amiss, but it depends very much on what else is happening as to how the gesture may be interpreted. We shall look later at the kinds of behaviour which tend to occur during attempts at deception.

A further problem is that self-conscious attempts to behave differently will almost inevitably appear unnatural and forced to others, so that the desired improvement in communication does not take place. It is often far better simply to register mentally the kind of behaviour that is likely to elicit from others the response you want and then behave naturally. What is in the back of your mind will still have some effect on what you do and you are therefore more likely to approach nearer to the kind of behaviour you want. Having said this, sometimes it is appropriate to make a conscious effort to change and, as we proceed, we shall try to identify these circumstances.

Embarrassment is a possible problem for shy or reserved people. As soon as they start looking closely at what they do, they become even less outgoing. If you are to derive the maximum benefit from this chapter, you will need to summon up your courage if you find yourself in this category.

Objectives

The basic objectives you should have (though you should, of course, add more specific objectives of your own to the list) are:

- Understanding why awareness, knowledge and expertise in using body language are important;
- Having an up-to-date picture of body language and a knowledge of the major research findings;
- Understanding the need for integration of spoken and body language in everyday encounters;
- Increasing perceptiveness in observing your own and other people's body language;
- Using body language more effectively in such contexts as meetings, negotiations, interviews, discussions and other face-to-face encounters.

Methods

We shall briefly examine each separate aspect of body language and then see how all of this information can be brought together to enable us to operate more effectively in a wide range of everyday encounters.

Firstly, *eye contact* or looking people in the eye when talking to them. Each person looks at the other for 25–75 per cent of the time in glances of 1–10 seconds. There is eye contact, or mutual gaze (when both are looking at each other's eyes) for shorter periods. There is more looking when listening and there is more looking if you like the other person (or the other person likes you). If people avoid eye contact, it may be a sign of absence of liking (but remember what was said earlier about taking other factors into account – he or she may simply not be a 'looker', just as some people are not 'kissers' or 'touchers' when greeting or saying goodbye).

The provision or withholding of eye contact communicates interpersonal attitudes. Giving it signals interest. It signals a wish to talk. Some people who wonder why someone 'pesters' them may unwittingly be sending out signals that they wish to talk when they do not.

Distance affects gaze. There is more mutual gaze with greater distance. That is one of the research conclusions which merely confirms common sense observation. Or is it? Why should we be more reluctant to establish eye contact the closer we are? Why should distance be a factor? So far research does not seem to have come up with a satisfactory answer.

Eye contact is important because it provides us with feedback on the reactions of others to what we have said or done. We use shifts of gaze to synchronise speech, often looking at the other person as we come to end what we have to say as if to convey the message, 'I've finished; now it's your turn.' People who 'talk across' others are often oblivious to such signals.

There are involuntary pupil responses which are worth watching for if you are close enough to another person to see them. It is known that the pupils of the eye dilate with interest. Since this response is quite clearly beyond the control of the individual, it is a phenomenon which has become of great interest to advertisers wanting to know what customers will respond positively towards. It may also be of some use to the salesperson facing a prospective client.

So eye contact has several uses. We use it to seek information, to show attention and interest, and to provide feedback during speech. Because many people do not like too much eye contact, it can also be used to dominate, threaten and influence others' reactions. More pleasantly, it can be used to invite people to talk. Whatever form it takes, it reveals much about our attitudes towards the people we are talking to.

How can you make practical use of all of this? For a start, you can become more acutely observant of people's use of eye contact. You can engage in a little more eye contact yourself – not a sudden increase, just a little more. When talking to people, you can use a direct, open gaze, rather than avoiding eye contact unless it is inescapable. You can try to be more sensitive to the amounts of eye contact that are appropriate in different contexts. You can try to have positive attitudes towards others for this will tend to encourage more eye contact quite naturally and unselfconsciously. Similarly, you can try to be a little more outgoing, if you are on the shy or reserved side. Take it gradually, though. Finally, always remember – a point that will be mentioned again before we are finished – integrate its use with all the other aspects of body language which we have yet to look at.

The second area we shall examine is that of *facial expression*. We use changes in facial expression in close combination with speech to modify or 'frame' what is said, showing humour, seriousness, importance and so on.

One interesting facial expression which seems to crop up in cultures around the world is that of the '*eyebrow flash*', a quick up and down movement of the eybrows, which is very common in greetings. It seems to signal both recognition of the person 'flashed' and pleasure at seeing them. Do you use it at all? It is a movement you might like to try sometime if you don't, but observe a few times how other people use it before you do.

There are also what are known as '*micromomentary*' expressions, which flick across the face so quickly many people miss them. They are said to be reliable indicators of concealed feelings. For example, someone might say they are pleased to meet you, but for a fraction of a second an expression of distaste replaces their insincere smile. Worth looking out for, wouldn't you say?

We exercise great control over our expressions, but some emotional reactions are difficult to conceal, such as disappointment at losing and elation at winning. The mouth and the eye areas convey most information, but forehead wrinkles, muscle twitches at the side of the face and the colour of the face (for instance, in blushing) can also tell us things.

Smiles are very important in communicating warmth, friendliness, willingness to talk, liking, pleasure, reassurance and so forth. The face can also, of course, show many other kinds of emotions and it is particularly important in creating first impressions because we make many quick judgments about people as soon as we meet them. Some researchers take the view that we make most of our important judgments about others in the first four or five minutes of knowing them. These judgments, once made, are not easily changed and we tend to remember those occasions on which we do change our mind about someone.

Facial expressions can be used to reinforce verbal messages, just as a smile accompanies a 'Well done!' a frown will go with a 'Don't do that!' If the facial expression conflicts with the verbal message, it is the *nonverbal* signal that will be believed. This often puzzles people who are habitual smilers and cannot understand why people will not take them seriously. The reason is simple. The smile which they see as mere civilised politeness (if they are aware of smiling at all) is perceived by others as light-heartedness.

We often use 'artefacts' like spectacles, jewellery, beards and make-up, to improve the appearance of our faces. The next time someone tries to tell you they don't think about their appearance, ask them how long they spent shaving that morning, or putting on make-up, or choosing their glasses when they bought them.

The face is also important in attempts at deception where it has, for instance, been observed that would-be deceivers tend to smile more than usual.

If you want to get the right kind of expression on to your face, you should smile more (but not too much), use the eyebrow flash in greetings, keep your chin up (common sense this, because a downcast face is simply harder to see and therefore interpret), show interest, make more changes in your facial expression (this signals liveliness) and make sure that your expression relates well to what you are saying.

Head nods are a third area of body language. Head nods accompanying listening act as a reinforcement and increase the behaviour nodded at. What this means is that, if you nod your head while someone else is talking, you will be encouraging them to talk more. Observe how TV interviewers use head nods to keep the people they are interviewing talking. Head nods also, of course, signal agreement, give permission to speak or (in the case of multiple nods) indicate a wish to speak. Researchers have observed that they seem to be co-ordinated between people who are talking and are not random. They produce a kind of 'gestural dance'.

Head position can be used to indicate attitudes, as in the 'head held high' position of someone who is rather haughty and aloof. Head movement can be used where speech is impossible, as, say, you might signal with a movement of the head that you wanted someone to come to you in a noisy factory. The head can be used to support what is being said, as in being shaken from side to side when disagreeing with someone.

Head movements have been observed to act as 'markers' in speech, punctuating, as it were, what is being said with small movements up, down or to one side. Watch a newsreader's head movements the next time the TV news is on and you should be able to see again a kind of 'dance' of the head taking place, with each movement occurring at a punctuation point in what is being said.

One interesting phenomenon observed in man and some animals is the head tilt when listening. The head is cocked to one side and this seems to signal special interest and attention. Dogs use it a lot, as do small children. Perhaps we adults might use it more to show that we are interested in what others have to say.

To use head nods and other head positions and movements more effectively, you should use head nods when acknowledging people socially, when speech is inappropriate, and to encourage others to talk more. Stop nodding when you want someone to stop talking. You may be surprised how quickly some people pick this signal up and do stop talking almost immediately after you have stopped nodding. The head can be swayed from side to side to express doubt. Again, the chin should be kept up, otherwise others will have some difficulty in interpreting the precise meaning of your head movements. It is also worth studying others' uses of head movements, especially on TV, where a great deal of body language can be watched closely without upsetting anyone.

An aspect of body language which has received a lot of attention from researchers is the area of *gestures and body movements*. Whilst it is true that gestures are not just made with the hands and can be made with the head, feet and other parts of the body, the hands are the most expressive.

Foot movements may provide 'leakage' of real feelings or of attempts at deception. For instance, you may ask someone a question to which their answer is a lie and it may not show in their face, but there may be restless shufflings of the feet which indicate some discomfort. Most people are not accomplished liars and do give themselves away with some form of leakage behaviour, more commonly in the lower half of the body than in the upper half.

Gestures indicate the general level of emotional tension and can be closely related to and supportive of speech. They may even replace speech in situations where speech is undesirable (for example, in a TV studio during a live transmission).

People talking tend to copy each other's gestures and postures (and other aspects of body language, for that matter) to produce a gestural synchrony and gestural echoes, in which if one person uses a gesture the other will use it also a few minutes later without realising it. You should never deliberately copy someone else's gestural pattern or style because, whilst they will respond favourably if they do not spot what you are doing, they will be very offended if they do spot you and will think that you are mimicking them in order to make fun of them.

There is a need for some liveliness in gestures, without becoming too wild about it. People who do not gesture tend also not to vary posture, speech patterns or other aspects of body language; they can be very lifeless. It is almost as if suppressing one aspect of body language automatically suppresses all others. This can be seen very clearly on body language courses where an exercise may deliberately manipulate just one aspect of body language, such as eye contact or head nods or smiles.

Gestures are often put into five classes:

- emblems (movements that are substitutes for words);
- illustrators (movements that accompany speech);
- regulators (movements that maintain or signal a change in a person's listening or speaking role);
- adaptors (movements such as scratching one's head or rubbing one's hands or fidding with objects and which therefore cast light on a person's emotional state); and
- affect displays (movements which more directly reveal emotions).

Gestures can be used to express openness, defensiveness, readiness, reassurance, confidence, nervousness, acceptance, expectancy and suspicion, among other things.

One interesting gesture is '*steepling*'. This is usually done sitting down and takes the form of the hands being held in front of the body with the finger tips of one hand each touching the corresponding finger tip on the other hand. It is used by eminent individuals to convey their high status and by those who think they are important to give that impression.

Gestures should be synchronised with speech. They should be synchronised with the gestures of others in a gestural dance, but not deliberately and obviously. You should use open gestures (like the hands held out in front of the body with the palms visible and the fingers spread out) rather than closed gestures (like clenching the fists or putting the hands in the pockets). You should avoid misleading gestures, as, for instance, when a woman wearing a short skirt crosses her legs and reveals an expanse of thigh. There may well be no intent to encourage, but it is a clear signal of such to many males. Similarly, a man may be misunderstood if he places what, for him, is a reassuring hand on a woman's shoulder. You might, however, like to experiment a little with steepling, especially in discussions and meetings, to see how others seem to interpret it.

Posture and stance are sometimes considered by researchers together with gestures and at least one has developed a theory of 'posture–gesture merging' which he claims can be used to identify people with simple body language styles. Such people, he argues, will tend to work better together than people whose body language styles are widely different. Posture–gesture merging has been used very effectively in team-building.

It is interesting to consider the different effects upon communication of standing, sitting or lying down. A presentation can be very different if it is made sitting down rather than standing up. Not usually as effective, but certainly different.

Posture conveys attitudes such as friendliness, hostility, superiority and inferiority. It can signal status and dominance by keeping the body erect and upright. It is usually measured on a tension–relaxation continuum, with formal postures being more tense and informal postures being more relaxed. Posture allows more leakage to be detected. Anxiety, for instance, is more likely to show in posture before it shows in the face. It is also an earlier indicator of status, aggression and dominance than other aspects of body language may be. Forward lean shows interest, sideways lean shows casualness and relaxation and backwards lean signals a wish to withdraw from what is going on around you. The next time you are in a meeting you might like to observe how lean is used to signal these various things.

If you want to use posture and stance more effectively, upright postures are generally perceived more positively than less upright ones. You should try to control your posture if you wish to reduce any leakage behaviour you may be displaying. You should use open postures, to go with your open gestures, and avoid barriers, like folding the arms. You should avoid too much tension in your posture and should avoid postural conflict with others. Don't imitate other people's postures obviously, but don't risk unnecessarily antagonising them by, say, slumping down in your chair when everyone else is sitting reasonably upright.

Proximity and orientation are important aspects of body language. Closeness or distance is related to the context in which things are happening, of course, and there are considerable cross-cultural variations in its use. Latin Americans tend to prefer to be closer to other people than Swedes, Scots and the English, for example. Changes in proximity can communicate the desire to initiate or terminate an encounter with people coming closer when they want to speak to you and beginning to move away when they feel the conversation should come to an end.

One researcher proposed four zones in the use of space:

- Zone 1, 0–0.5m, the *intimate* zone;
- Zone 2, 0.5–1.2m, the *personal* zone;
- Zone 3, 1.2–3m, the *social-consultive* zone;
- Zone 4, from 3m outwards, the *public* zone.

Each zone could also be divided into close and not close areas.

Competition and co-operation are influenced by proximity and orientation. In competitive situations, people tend to adopt face-to-face positions and in co-operative situations people tend to place themselves side by side. In most contexts, people adopt indirect orientations – somewhere between face-to-face and side-by-side – because these give them the most choice about how they are going to interact. If the encounter becomes more friendly, they can then more easily move closer together and if it becomes less friendly, they can more easily move away and turn away without this becoming too obvious.

There seems to be an area or 'bubble' of personal space that we carry around with us and into which we do not like people intruding. If they do, as for example in a lift, we 'freeze' or get out of the situation as soon as we can. The exception to this reaction is if people are perceived as 'non-persons'. Examples of non-persons would be waiters in restaurants, when a confidential conversation between two people may continue despite the fact that the waiter can hear it. Other examples might be caretakers, window cleaners, postmen, cleaners and patients whose condition is discussed in their hearing by nurses and doctors.

The concept of defensible space is an interesting one and research has shown that people are happier living in places where they have space that others may not enter and happier working in places where they have some territory of their own. In open-plan offices, for example, or libraries or trains, people will often place objects like coats, briefcases or papers around themselves to signal to others that the territory so marked should not be invaded. Bodily orientation is also used in places like bars by groups of people to indicate to others that they should not intrude upon the group's territory. This can be very inconvenient if such markers are near the serving area and prevent others being served.

You can make more effective use of proximity and orientation if you encourage rather than discourage proximity. You should encourage the use of indirect orientations, especially in interviews. You should keep territorial markers to a minimum. Try not to treat others as non-persons. Keep interactions open as often as possible. Be sensitive to cross-cultural differences in the use of proximity and orientation.

Probably the most sensitive area of body language, both literally and metaphorically, is *bodily contact*. The most common forms in business contexts are handshakes, pats on the back, holding the arm above the elbow (often when shaking hands as a reinforcement of the gesture) and the guiding hand at someone's back. There are, though, great cross-cultural variations in the amount of touching that people are prepared to allow. In countries like Britain and Japan, it is usually very little. In African and Arab countries there is much more touching permitted.

Touching is most common in greetings and farewells and even the most fleeting and casual bodily contact has been found to be significant. In one interesting experiment, people who went into a library were either handed their tickets without any physical contact with the librarian or they were given them into their hand with the librarian's hand briefly touching theirs. Afterwards, all those who had visited the library were asked to rate the librarian on a number of dimensions. Those who had been touched, even though extremely briefly, consistently rated the librarian more positively and as being warmer, more friendly, more intelligent, better at the job and so on.

Touching is more likely when giving information or advice than when asking for it, when giving an order than when receiving one and when trying to persuade than when being persuaded. It is more likely during leisure time than working hours, when expressing enthusiasm than when listening to someone else's enthusiasm and when listening to someone's worries than when expressing one's own. There are also forms of self-touching, such as stroking the chin, scratching the head, grooming the hair and rubbing the nose.

Hugging is thought by many researchers to be very important. In families where hugging is a normal part of behaviour among the members, children tend to be better balanced emotionally, better mixers socially and generally more outgoing and at ease with others. The adults also exhibit fewer signs of stress or emotional instability.

It is less easy to suggest how you might make better use of bodily contact than it is to suggest improvements in the use of other aspects of body language, but one or two possibilities are to use handshakes in greetings more often, to remember that pats on the back can be literal as well as metaphoric and to avoid shying away from brief physical contact in dealings with others. Whatever is done, however, needs to be appropriate and there is no point in trying to encourage more bodily contact with someone who clearly does not welcome it. Men have to be particularly careful in this regard when dealing with women, although men do not usually mind the occasional contact when initiated by a woman. It remains an area for the exercise of extreme care and to let others dictate what they feel is best for them.

Appearance and physique are important factors in communicating information about ourselves to others. Aspects like body build and condition, height, physical attractiveness and clothes can all be manipulated as a part of self-presentation. The effects of appearance upon judgment are not always what might be expected. For instance, a considerable amount of research shows that more attractive women are treated more leniently than others if they are in court facing charges. However, some research has shown that this general rule does not apply if the offence committed was one in which the woman actually exploited her attractiveness, as in, for example, certain kinds of confidence trick.

Appearance and physique also play an important role in the first impressions we form of others. It would be a bold, or reckless, person who would turn up for a selection interview for a job without paying careful attention to this aspect of self-presentation.

If you wish to make the most of your appearance, you should observe yourself and try to see yourself as others see you. Experiment with variations in clothing and note the effects. Experiment with different hair styles and note the effects. Slim if you are overweight, though this is often easier said than done. Pay particular attention to the care of the face and skin. Finally, observe other people for possible ideas about styles you might like to try.

The *relationship between body language and speech* is one which should not be overlooked. Variations in stress, intonation, pitch, volume and timing can all affect the final outcome of the communication taking place. Speech errors may be indicative of nervousness or attempts to deceive. Certainly we make judgments about people if there are too many speech errors – or even if there are too few. If there are none at all, the person may be perceived as being too glib.

Some *cross-cultural variations in body language* have already been noted. Others worth mentioning are that Greeks stare more in public places. Swedes look less often but for longer and Arabs are very dependent upon eye contact when conversing. The Japanese look at other people very little. They keep a straight face with a slight smile. They make more use of smiles in greetings and in business and formal settings than Europeans. They bow frequently and the depth of the bow is related to the perceived status of the other. Higher status people receive deeper bows. Italians and Arabs stand closer to each other when conversing. Germans stand further apart. Latins engage in more touching behaviour than others. The tone of the voice is particularly important to Arabs, as is the smell of the other person.

Of the few aspects of body language that are universally present, pretty well regardless of culture, the main ones seem to be smiles (even babies born blind from birth smile when pleased), the eyebrow flash in greetings, and expressions of such emotional reactions as joy, surprise, fear, anger, sadness and disgust. Behaviour in greetings also reveals many similarities. There is close proximity with a direct orientation, eyebrow flash, eye contact, bodily contact in the form of presenting the palm of the hand for a handshake, and a head toss or head nod in the form of a bow.

This chapter has been, inevitably, a quick survey of the main aspects of body language and of the things we might do in order to improve our use of them, but it might be useful to finish by taking some everyday situations and to suggest which particular aspects of body language are important in them. There are many similarities, but there are also some subtle but important differences between, say, the way you run an interview and the way you run a meeting.

In interviews a 90° orientation is preferable (that is, the participants do not sit opposite each other, nor side by side, but in a position half way between the two). There should be reinforcing and encouraging head nods by the interviewer, encouraging smiles, limited body movements so as not to disturb the interviewee's train of thought and a reasonably relaxed body posture. A soft voice quality should be used and there should be more looking by the interviewer to encourage the interviewee to speak at greater length.

In meetings, it is important to have an appropriate table and room size and to avoid confrontational positions between known antagonists. Round or oval tables are best for most meeting purposes. There should be limited body movement and an attentive posture to those expressing opposing points of view. This will tend to soften the edge of their opposition. There should be increased eye contact especially between opponents, since greater looking promotes greater liking and lessens antagonism over time. There should be attempts to limit distracting hesitations and speech errors in order to give the meeting a reasonable feeling of pace.

Negotiations and bargaining benefit best from an informal atmosphere, avoidance of confrontational orientations, friendly facial expressions, soft voice quality and similarity in dress. This last is important because people who look alike tend to act alike and to agree with each other. Attentiveness should be indicated through nonverbal cues such as head nods and slight forward lean and there should be limited body movements.

Successful performance in briefings requires you to limit the distance from your audience, to use an upright posture and to face the audience the whole time. Briefings call for more body movement and use of gesture, controlled and not wandering. There has to be some 'projection' of facial expressions and of the voice. There should be eye contact as frequently as possible with as many members of the audience as possible. Speech errors should be very carefully controlled. Your appearance should be more formal than informal. You have to be a little larger than life in a briefing, the more so as the numbers increase.

Training sessions are very much the same as briefings, except that where the group numbers less than about fifteen, the approach should be more informal and friendly to encourage others to participate more.

In sales environments, there should be appropriate bodily contact (certainly an introductory handshake where possible), as close a proximity as the customer seems comfortable with and a forward leaning posture. A 90° orientation removes any threat the customer might feel from a close proximity. There should be plenty of smiles, eye contact and rather more speech errors to avoid sounding too smooth and well-rehearsed. A reasonably formal appearance is also usual.

To improve relationships with subordinates, some body contact may help (encouraging pats on the back can be literal as well as metaphoric in appropriate circumstances). Close proximity, where permitted by the subordinate, a relaxed posture and side-by-side orientations wherever practicable. There should be frequent head nods to encourage the other to talk, limited gestures, smiles and increased eye contact.

To improve relationships with superiors, it is best to let the other set the general tone and pattern for the use of body language, although smoother interactions can still be assisted with increased use of head nods and eye contact and similarity in dress (avoiding obvious imitation). People do tend to respond more favourably to people they feel are more like themselves than to those who clearly are not.

Before we leave body language, we should consider its use in a situation where it would not initially seem relevant and that is when we are using the telephone. Since you cannot be seen, what is the relevance of body language? You only have to watch someone on the phone to realise that it is, in fact, highly relevant. We seem to need posture changes, gestures, changes in the voice and even the face just as much when we cannot see the other person as when we can; perhaps even more. To use the phone more effectively, you should pay greater attention to the nonverbal aspects of speech about which we spoke earlier. There should be frequent vocal 'head nods' – with a 'yes', 'uhuh', or 'mmm' – to indicate attentiveness. Special care should be taken with the tone of voice because this can be distorted over the phone. The same applies to the volume of your speech.

Evaluation

Consider the questions we posed at the beginning of this chapter. Would you change your answers at all in the light of what you have read? What sort of answers would the research suggest? Well, there is only one way to find out. Let us look at the questions again here. The answers are provided, but make your own consideration first.

Do not read on until you have done this.

1 Why don't people look at each other in lifts and on the tube?

Answer – Eye contact when close to people is too powerful to be endured for long, but no one quite knows why.

2 Why don't people smile as they walk to work in the morning?

Answer – People in small towns and villages often do. It is the large city which seems to have wiped the smile off our faces. Why don't you put it back on again tomorrow and see what happens?

3 Why do people nod when listening to someone else?

Answer – As we have seen, it has the effect of making them talk more. You find out more about them that way.

4 Why do so many people fold their arms or put their hands in their pockets when making a presentation?

Answer – Insecurity and defensiveness, perhaps caused by a lack of knowledge of the subject, poor preparation or lack of rehearsal – or all three.

5 Why do people lean forward when they are interested?

Answer – For a start, you can hear the other person a little more clearly, but no one knows the real answer. We know that they do and that it works.

6 What is a comfortable distance between two people when they are standing talking?

Answer – Zone 2 (0.5–1.2 m) – probably the 'not close' area.

7 Why do so many people not like being touched by other people?

Answer – *Some cultures are more 'touch' cultures than others and some families are more 'touch' families than others, perhaps for cultural or personality reasons.*

8 What can you tell about a person from the way they dress?

Answer – *Many things. You can make reasonable predictions about their sex, their job, their age, their general personality. Next time you and someone else are in a waiting situation play the guessing game on these and any other dimensions you choose based on appearance. It works best if you get the chance to check up afterwards.*

9 Why do some people 'talk across' other people in a discussion?

Answer – *Either downright insensitivity or a simple failure to respond to nonverbal cues such as eye contact.*

10 How would you use your voice to encourage someone to trust you?

Answer – *In a word – softly. Who is going to trust someone who talks loud, fast and with many speech errors?*

Ongoing

You will find that your skill in using body language will continue to improve if you carry out some of the following activities regularly:

- Observe other people's use of body language and try to observe the various aspects – eye contact, facial expression, gestures, orientation and so on – independently. Always remember, though, to look at the body language in the whole context before making any judgments on the basis of it.
- Try the smiling exercise mentioned earlier. As you go out one morning, keep a cheerful expression on your face. Smile briefly – don't do it for long – at those whose eyes you catch. Don't you feel better for it?

- Try nodding more when people are speaking to you. Do they talk for longer and reveal more?
- Observe your friends' gestures? Who has favourites, like grooming the hair or stroking the chin?
- Try using a more erect posture. After one week, do you feel better?
- Observe an open plan office, in which all are supposed to be equal. Can you tell who the higher status individuals are? How?
- Observe people telephoning. Can you tell anything from their body language about who they are speaking to and what they are speaking about?
- Observe people from a range of ethnic groups. How does their body language vary?
- Watch part of a film on TV with the sound turned down. What can you tell about the plot from the body language?
- Next time you suspect someone is trying to deceive you, what are the body language cues that aroused your suspicions?

Completion checklist

At the end of this chapter you should be able to answer the following questions:

1. How much of the impact of a face-to-face message does one American researcher attribute to nonverbal communication?
2. What is one of the main reasons why many people experience problems in using body language?
3. What is the 'eyebrow flash'?
4. Give two examples of 'artefacts' used in body language.
5. Which aspect of body language in particular may provide 'leakage' of real feelings?
6. What is a 'gestural echo'?
7. What is 'steepling'?
8. Which aspects of body language are thought to be universal?
9. Which aspects of body language are particularly important in meetings?
10. How do we use body language when making a telephone call?
11. If the spoken word and body language conflict, which is believed?

Conclusion

Body language is a difficult subject for some people to talk about, probably because for the most part we use it intuitively and unconsciously and once you look at that kind of activity a certain embarrassment and self-consciousness develops. Hopefully, after reading this chapter, you will have no such inhibitions and you will be willing to try out some of the Ongoing exercises described above.

So long as you do not make changes in your body language too obviously and too suddenly or dramatically, you should find that it is possible, over a period of time, to use the skills more effectively. The rewards should be more effective communication with others, better relationships and a general sense of confidence and well-being.

Review what you have learned from this chapter before you go to sleep tonight.

12

EFFECTIVE MEETINGS

Modern organisations cannot function efficiently without meetings. If people are to participate fully in an organisation and influence its development, they must meet, despite what cynics would have us believe. An organisation which has no meetings either is, or soon will be, a dictatorship.

This is not to argue that there are not too many meetings. Clearly, there can be. Nor is it to argue that we cannot use meetings more effectively. Clearly we can.

Review

The next time you attend a meeting, ask yourself the following questions:

1 Is everybody present clear as to what the meeting is about?
2 Are there too few or too many people at the meeting?
3 Is there anybody present who does not need to be there?
4 Is the room in which the meeting is being held the right size and does it have the right facilities?
5 Does the meeting last longer than it needs to?
6 Is the person in the chair good at the task of chairing a meeting?
7 Are minutes being taken? Do they need to be taken? Are they being taken in the form most appropriate for the needs of those attending the meeting?
8 Is there an agenda? Does there need to be one? Are the items in the most suitable order?
9 Does everyone who wants to speak get the chance to?

10 Do any of those attending the meeting engage in disruptive behaviour (for example, talking amongst themselves, disagreeing for sake of disagreeing, riding a hobby horse or talking for the sake of talking)?

Write down your responses to the questions. We shall return to them at the end of the chapter.

Problems

The problems we experience with meetings are many and varied and, since there are so many, the most convenient thing to do will be to list them:

- The meeting becomes entangled in its own procedures and people argue about how the meeting is being conducted rather than what it is about;

- There are too many amendments proposed to the proposition being discussed;

- There are too many points of order raised;

- There is confusion among those attending the meeting about what exactly has been decided;

- There is disruptive behaviour by one or more of those attending the meeting;

- The opening and the closing of the meeting are uncertain and hesitant;

- The meeting avoids making decisions;

- The meeting is badly run;

- The meeting starts late;

- The meeting wanders from the point;

- Some of those present have 'hidden' objectives they wish to achieve (for example, someone wishes to discuss a topic not on the agenda, someone wants to be regarded as an opinion leader or someone wants to undermine the authority of the chair) and these hinder progress;

- There is a lack of opportunity to participate, whether because there are simply too many people there or the chair does not allow sufficient time for participation;

- Conflict between those attending the meeting is allowed or even encouraged by the chair;

- A search for compromise and consensus reduces morale;

- The chair is weak and does not exercise enough control over the meeting;

- The meeting lasts too long;

- The wrong people are present at the meeting;

- There are too many meetings;

- The meeting is taking place for the sake of meeting;

- There are not enough people present to reach a quorum (the minimum number of people who must be present in certain formal meetings);

- Those attending have not prepared themselves properly for the meeting, perhaps by not having studied carefully the papers sent out before the meeting;

- There is too much paperwork (which might also have led to the previous point);

- Meetings have a high cost. Look around the meeting you are attending. Add up the annual salaries of those present. Divide by the average number of hours worked in a year. This gives you a cost per meeting hour. Multiply by how many hours the meeting lasts. Frightening, isn't it? And that is only one meeting!

Objectives

The basic objectives you should have (though you should, of course, add more specific objectives of your own to the list) are:

- Defining objectives for meetings;
- Demonstrating a knowledge of the basic principles of the effective conduct and use of meetings;
- Chairing meetings more effectively;
- Identifying the main causes of meetings failing to reach agreement;
- Participating effectively in meetings;
- Following the conventions and procedures appropriate to various kinds of meetings.

Methods

Before any useful meeting can be held, you have to satisfy certain preconditions and be clear about the purpose of the meeting. The first question you should ask yourself is: Is a meeting really necessary? There is no point in calling people together for a meeting if there is no real need for it or if its purpose could be better achieved, and more quickly, in some other way. For instance, if all you want to do is give a few people some simple pieces of information, a circulated memo may do the trick. Or if you prefer the more human touch and the staff concerned all work on the same floor of the building, you might go round and see them.

If you decide that a meeting is necessary, you have to be clear about its purpose. There can be many reasons for holding a meeting. Some of the more common ones are:

– To co-ordinate activities.

– To build morale.

– To provide a framework within which risks can be shared.

- To brief people on the current state of an organisation's affairs.
- To solve problems.
- To call people together to consult them.
- To exchange information.
- To make policy for an organisation.
- To enable people to air grievances and let off steam.
- To persuade people to agree with a point of view or agree with a set of proposals.
- To explore an issue.
- To achieve 'hidden' objectives of the kind exemplified earlier.

Once your purpose is clear, you have a better chance of meeting the other preconditions. You must decide what type of meeting it is to be. There are at least six types:

- **Executive or command meetings.** These are best suited to giving information when not much discussion of it is expected or necessary.
- **Discussion or consultative or advisory meetings.** In this kind of meeting, it is more important that people have a chance to consider all the issues rather than reach firm decisions.
- **Colleague meetings.** These will discuss matters of common interest on the basis of all the members present being equals and will then make decisions for action.
- **Committee meetings.** These are general purpose discussion and decision making meetings and they need skilful chairing and accurate minutes.
- **Bargaining or negotiating or trading meetings.** These are usually (and perhaps best) kept informal, low in numbers attending and held in more comfortable surroundings. If you wish to create conflict, the reverse will apply.
- **Progress or review meetings.** These are usually held to check that everybody has done everything they were given to do at the

previous meeting and to set new tasks for the period immediately ahead. Everyone involved needs to be present or send a deputy to report back to them. People may wish to attend who do not strictly need to, for instance, in order to keep themselves or their department up-to-date on the general progress of a project.

You should consider how formal the meeting is to be. The more formally it is conducted, the greater the need for clear rules of procedure and debate and for a person to take the chair. Formal meetings also have a greater need for a written record of what happened, in the form of minutes. Informal meetings can do away with most of these things and may even, if they are small, be able to operate quite satisfactorily without someone in the chair.

You have to determine the content of the meeting. If there is to be an agenda, what kinds of items will appear on it? How large should the meeting be, bearing in mind that the larger a meeting is, the less opportunity, generally, there is for people to participate fully. Who should be present? Is it possible to restrict attendance only to those who need to be there? Or does tact demand that some people have to be asked for form's sake?

Where is the meeting to be held? The setting is more important than many people realise. It will not help if the room is too large or too small for the numbers attending, nor if it is too hot or too cold, nor if the seating is too comfortable or too uncomfortable. Even the shape of the table matters. Seat two opposing groups on opposite sides of a table and you will get noticeably more antagonism between them than if everybody is seated around a round or oval table. They will still sit in their separate 'camps', but there will not be the same amount of conflict generated.

When the meeting is to be held is also an important consideration. It is not a good idea to hold meetings just before or soon after lunch. People's minds are on other things, just as they will be if you call them too early in the day or too late in the day. 9.30 am and 2 pm seem to be popular starting times. Both allow people to clear their desks of urgent matters for the morning or afternoon and both allow plenty of time for detailed discussion of complex issues if required.

Who should take the chair is probably the most important consideration of all and yet the one that is usually given least thought. The most senior person present takes the chair. But the most senior person may not be the best at conducting meetings. It is pointless selecting people on the basis of position or status when you should be selecting them on the basis of skill. You will have to do the best you can on this point, although you may be able to do nothing at all.

You will need to decide if minutes are to be taken and, if so, who is going to do it and how detailed the minutes need to be. It is best to select someone who will not have to take an active part in the meetings to take the minutes; it is almost impossible to play an active part in a meeting and take minutes at the same time. Minutes are best kept to a simple record of decisions taken, with perhaps a brief explanation of what the item was about if necessary. Either that or you should prepare a word-for-word account of what was said. Anything in between will always cause problems as people dispute the way the minute taker has interpreted what was meant in order to express things more concisely.

You should be clear as to who is responsible for making all these arrangements and any others that must be taken care of. If it is you, there is no problem. If you are delegating the task to someone else, make your requirements crystal clear and as detailed as necessary. Then check that everything has been done to specification.

Once everything is ready and the time of the meeting arrives, what happens? Many people are a little unsure of how to get things started. This need not be complicated. The chair checks the time and quorum (if necessary) and announces the start of the meeting. The agenda is read if there is one or, more usually, is taken as having been read. Apologies for absence (if any) are taken. The chair announces the first item on the agenda.

The agenda can take several forms, but a typical one for a formal committee meeting might be:

1 Apologies.
2 Minutes of the last meeting.
3 Minutes of any sub-committees.
4 Matters arising (but not usually in local authority committee meetings, though it may depend on the chair).
5 Major items.
6 Minor items.
7 Routine minor items.
8 Confidential items.
9 Any other business (but not usually in local authority committee meetings, though it may depend on the chair).

10 Date of next meeting (if it is not part of a regular cycle of meetings and if one is required).

For some kinds of meetings, it is worth having a quorum, that is, the number of people who must be present before a meeting can legally make decisions. It can be an important safeguard against filibustering tactics by a militant minority who then make major decisions after most of the other people have got fed up with the meeting dragging on and have left.

In more formal meetings it is usual to put propositions forward in the form of *motions*, which is what a proposal is before it is decided upon. Once it is passed, it becomes a *resolution*. The convention is that motions are phrased positively rather than negatively. In other words that they propose to do something rather than not to do something. The reason for this is that negatively worded statements are more difficult to understand. If there are motions, there will almost certainly also be amendments to these motions. Motions can be amended by:

- omitting words;
- substituting words;
- inserting words;
- combining any of these.

An amendment may not directly contradict the sense of a motion, for the simple reason that, if that is what a group of those present desire, all they have to do is vote against the motion when it comes to the vote.

At the end of the meeting, when all the business has been conducted, the chair will declare the meeting closed. No one may then raise any further business until the next meeting.

If, as a meeting proceeds, you wish to participate more effectively, there are various ways in which you can do this. You should first of all find out as much as you can about what has happened at previous meetings. You should find out who will be present and find out as much as you can about them. Identify the opinion leaders and make sure you understand the 'politics'.

If you have a meeting to attend, you should always be properly prepared. You should define your terms of reference in attending the meeting. Assess the audience at the meeting. Set yourself objectives for the meeting. Beforehand, make sure you have collected all the information you will need to achieve your objectives.

During the meeting, make notes of what other people say. Use key words and phrases rather than trying to get every word down. This helps if you wish to bring a meeting back on course and the chair does not appear willing to do so. You can say something like, 'Surely, what we are really here to discuss is . . .' and refer authoritatively to the correct part of your notes.

If you are going to make a contribution to a fairly formal meeting, have notes to speak from (see Chapter 10, page 110). Find something to speak on early in the meeting before the point where you wish to make your main contribution. Early participation helps to break the ice and give confidence. If you are presenting a case, remember the value of visual aids. Identify common ground between yourself and your listeners and don't stray further from it than you need to.

Don't forget the importance of body language in meetings. It might be worth re-stating the main points:

- Establish eye contact with your audience;
- Use appropriate facial expressions. Don't forget the power of the smile;
- Use head nods when listening. Keep your head up when speaking;
- Use gestures to emphasise points. Prefer open and expressive gestures;
- Prefer upright to slouching posture;
- Sit near the front;
- Face your audience directly when speaking;
- Remember appearance can influence who is attended to and who is not;
- Be sensitive to timing and synchronisation;
- Never be afraid to pause to let a point sink in;
- Observe others' use of body language in order to identify which kinds are most effective.

Whatever the meeting (except a very small and informal one) and whatever the reason for calling it, the most important person during its course is the chair. It is the function of the chair to preserve order, to enforce any rules of procedure the organisation has, to rule on disputed matters, to maintain the policy of the organisation and prevent irrelevant discussion.

The person in the chair should possess certain personal qualities. He or she should be clear thinking and not easily swayed by emotional or irrational considerations. The chair needs a sense of humour and has to be able to control his or her temper. There is evidence that people who are slightly inward looking make better chairs than those who are more outgoing and extrovert.

Different kinds of meetings require different styles of chairing. Policy making meetings require a consultative style. Problem solving meetings need a democratic style, where everybody is encouraged to participate as equals. Meetings called to air grievances require a facilitative style to allow things to come out into the open. Few, if any, meetings will benefit from an authoritarian style.

If there is a 'hidden' agenda of 'hidden' objectives, the chair should be someone who is sufficiently perceptive to be aware of this and be able to take steps to ensure that it does not undermine the effectiveness of the meeting. Bringing it out into the open often frightens people away from the 'hidden' agenda.

Disruption can take many forms, from occasional sniping remarks to a direct refusal to obey a request from the chair to sit down and be quiet. Sometimes it may be necessary to be firm and even blunt with disruptors. Sometimes it helps if the chair restates the objectors' points to ensure they know the chair understands their point of view. This may also make some people realise they have a weak case for the meeting's attention. Occasionally it may be necessary to adjourn the meeting for a short while to allow everyone to cool down.

It may help if the chair understands the main causes of conflict which lead people to be disruptive. People are more likely to be disruptive if they feel they are being unreasonably prevented from achieving a goal important to them. Someone who simply does not fit into a group is more likely to be disruptive. There is likely to be some truculence by long-established members of an organisation against people they regard as newcomers or 'foreigners'. A small group of people who see themselves as being different from the larger group of which they are a part are more likely to be troublesome as they seek to assert their identity. Good old-fashioned communication failure is often the cause for disruptive behaviour.

An important function of the chair, of course, is to help the meeting to reach decisions. He or she needs to be sensitive to the signs that people are ready to decide and needs an appropriate method of recording that decision. Sometimes a show of hands will be appropriate, whilst on other occasions it may be necessary to have a ballot. Above all, the chair must ensure that the meeting understands the decisions it has made.

Perhaps we are now in a position to look at the list of problems with meetings which we had at the beginning of this chapter and suggest possible solutions:

- Becoming entangled in procedure.
  Possible solution: Simplify the rules.
- Too many amendments.
  Possible solution: Establish priority order.
- Too many points of order.
  Possible solution: Limit them to points of procedure.
- Confusion over what has been decided.
  Possible solution: Chair to summarise and clarify the decision.
- Disruptive behaviour.
  Possible solution: Adjourn briefly.
- Uncertain opening and closing.
  Possible solution: Step-by-step procedure for chair to follow.
- Decisions are avoided.
  Possible solution: Request a vote.
- Meetings are badly run.
  Possible solution: Change or train chair.
- Meetings start late.
  Possible solution: Secretary to remind chair.
- Meetings wander from the point.
  Possible solution: Change or train chair.
- Hidden objectives hinder progress.
  Possible solution: Bring them out into the open.
- Lack of chance to participate.
  Possible solution: Reduce the numbers who have to attend.
- Conflict is encouraged.
  Possible solution: Change or train chair.
- Consensus and compromise reduce morale.
  Possible solution: Find a chair who can give a stronger lead.
- Weak chairing.
  Possible solution: Change or train chair.
- Meetings last too long.
  Possible solution: Set a time limit.
- The wrong people attend.
  Possible solution: Change the attendance list.

- There are too many meetings.
  Possible solution: Review the meetings list.
- Meetings take place for the sake of it.
  Possible solution: Delete unnecessary meetings from the list.
- Inability to reach a quorum.
  Possible solution: Remind people in advance.
- Poor preparation by members attending.
  Possible solution: Send papers out a little earlier.
- Too much paperwork.
  Possible solution: Pre-meeting between chair and secretary to try to reduce it.
- The high cost of meetings.
  Possible solution: Review the meetings list regularly and seek fewer and shorter meetings.

Evaluation

After you have been trying to put the guidance and advice given in this chapter into effect for about a month, ask yourself the questions you asked in the Review section at the beginning of the chapter. Do you feel you get more satisfactory answers this time? Hopefully, you will.

Ongoing

You will find that your skill in conducting and participating in meetings of all kinds will continue to improve if you carry out some of the following activities regularly:

- Every so often when you are attending a meeting ask yourself the questions you were asked in the Review section at the beginning of this chapter.
- Make an action list of the things you have learned from this chapter that you intend to put into practice. Check the list occasionally to see if you really are putting the items into practice and whether new items need to be added.

- After a meeting, draw up an action sheet listing, in columns, the agenda item, a brief description of it, the decision, the action required, by whom it is required, when it is required by and when the action is completed.
- Draw up a contribution rate chart for your next meeting. Column 1 is the name of the participant. Column 2 is a tally of his or her contributions to the meeting. Column 3 is the total of the tallies in each case. Who contributes most often? Who contributes least? Is this as it should be? If you can, try putting all the high contributors into one group and all the low contributors into another. What happens when you put everybody back together again for a discussion or meeting? You should find that the high contributors now contribute less (because they have had other high contributors to compete with) and the low contributors now contribute more (for the first time, they have had a real chance to talk). This should give a better balance to discussions in future meetings.
- List as many alternatives to meetings as you can. How many of them would help you to reduce the number of meetings you have to attend without reducing your effectiveness in the organisation?

Completion checklist

At the end of this chapter you should be able to answer the following questions:

1. How many of the problems encountered in meetings can you list?
2. What are some of the more common reasons for holding meetings?
3. List the six types of meetings described.
4. What is probably the most important consideration of all in holding a meeting?
5. Which items appear and in which order on a typical agenda for a formal meeting?
6. List four ways in which motions at meetings can be amended.
7. List the qualities desirable in the person taking the chair.

Conclusion

Meetings may sometimes be a nuisance, but if you can learn to conduct and participate in them more effectively they may come to be less of a nuisance. If people would give some attention to getting right the kinds of considerations we have discussed in this chapter, we might all find meetings easier to bear and even begin to enjoy them a little.

One thing is certain, if only a little more thought were given to the selection of a person to take the chair, this, more than anything else, could make a major contribution towards improving the effectiveness of meetings.

Review what you have learned from this chapter before you go to sleep tonight.

13

MANAGING PEOPLE

People are the most important asset any organisation has. If they are not managed efficiently and effectively, the costs will be considerable. There will be costs not only in the making of avoidable mistakes and consequent loss of business, but also in the failure to exploit fully the potential that lies within people. It is this potential which can greatly increase an organisation's profitability and effectiveness.

A manager, it is often said, is someone who works through other people. It is vital, therefore, that managers should raise their skills in the management of the people for whom they are responsible to the highest level of proficiency of which they are capable.

People management is yet another skill which is not taught in our educational system. So, if you have to manage other people as a part of your work or leisure activities – which in one way or another means most of us – this chapter is for you.

Review

Make a list of the people who report directly to you. If you do not have people reporting to you, make a list of the people you work with or the people you live with. Answer these questions about them:

1 How are they important to you in doing your work or running your life?
2 How often do you see them?
3 Do they usually come to see you or do you go to see them?
4 How often do you see them other than about something they have done wrong or not done at all?
5 Do you ever praise them for doing things well?

6 Do you know what their hobbies or interests are?
7 Do you know what family (or friends) they have?
8 Do you ever mix with them socially?
9 How would they like you to change the way you do your work (or run your life) so that they could do (or run) theirs more effectively? Do you know?
10 What system do you have for them to come up with ideas to improve the organisation's efficiency and effectiveness?

Now make a list of the people who report to these people and answer the questions again. Is it as easy or more difficult? If it is more difficult, why?

Problems

One major problem in managing people better stems from the simple fact that very few of us ever receive any training in the skills of people management. We join organisations or go into a career originally to carry out the work involved in that career, be it teaching, making cars, dentistry, digging coal or selling washing powder. Before too long, if we show promise we are promoted. We keep getting promoted, if we are any good, to jobs which require less and less in the way of technical knowledge and practical ability and more and more in the way of managerial skills, amongst which the most important is managing people.

Very often, as the last exercise might have demonstrated, we simply do not know enough about the people we manage to be able to organise their work in the way they are best able to do it. We tend to assume that there is a right way of doing things, but very often the people we manage could tell us, if they were asked, that there is more than one way.

To a greater or lesser extent, people are unpredictable. It is not always wise to assume that everyone will react in the same way to an instruction or a request or even to an apparently harmless action. I recall some years ago, having been recently promoted to a senior post in a college, going along to the library to book its film theatre for a showing to a class. I wanted to book several showings as there were several classes and I wanted to plan my classes some time ahead.

The system was a simple one. You entered the details in the diary and then signed your name for each entry. I did this. Some days later

I was buttonholed by a much older and longer serving but junior member of staff. What did I mean by booking so many showings and so far in advance and who did I think I was impressing by flaunting my position?

The first point I had an answer for – I wanted to be sure of having the theatre when I needed it. The latter point had me beaten. It turned out that I had offended against unwritten rules that the theatre, because there was such competition to use it, was not normally booked for more than two weeks in advance. On the second point, it emerged that, in my normal way, I had underlined my signature. This had been taken as an attempt to bypass the normal fortnight's gentlemen's agreement because of my senior position. It was taken as a warning off signal to other members of staff because the underlining had been seen not for what it was, simple habit, but as a way of emphasising each entry. I have never since underlined my signature.

The problems we have with managing people can be much more subtle and pervasive than problems encountered in the exercise of other skills, but we shall see how many solutions we can identify for the problems that may arise.

Objectives

The basic objectives you should have (though you should, of course, add more specific objectives of your own to the list) are:

- Defining objectives for managing people;
- Demonstrating a knowledge of the basic principles of the effective management of people;
- Understanding the nature of different roles at work;
- Identifying the main causes of problems that can arise in the management of people;
- Leading people more effectively;
- Understanding the importance of effective delegation;
- Motivating people more effectively.

Methods

We first need to know what the skills are that we use to manage people with and how they relate to management skills generally. One possible way to classify managerial skills is to divide them into *intellectual or analytical* skills (or what you might broadly call technical skills) and *social or communicative skills* (or what you might call people skills). A typical list of the two kinds of skills might look like this:

A Intellectual/Analytical Skills

- Studying and learning the work;
- Investigating and researching;
- Overviewing (i.e., obtaining an overall picture);
- Diagnosing and fault-finding;
- Analysing and criticising (i.e., looking for deficiencies and merits);
- Judging (i.e., making judgments);
- Deciding;
- Initiating and creating;
- Planning and setting objectives;
- Forecasting, budgeting and allocating resources;
- Designing systems and procedures;
- Controlling and programming;
- Evaluating and assessing (e.g., achievements, people);
- Monitoring and checking;
- Problem-solving and troubleshooting.

B Social/Communicative Skills

- Having appropriate attitudes (i.e., those suiting the organisational climate);
- Motivating self and others;
- Having an acceptable personality;
- Having charisma or presence (not an essential quality);
- Leading and inspiring others;
- Organising;
- Directing;
- Supervising;
- Selling, convincing and persuading;
- Promoting and publicising;
- Instructing and training;
- Developing and coaching others;
- Competing and being assertive;
- Empathising (seeing situations from others' viewpoints);
- Relating to others and establishing rapport;
- Consulting and being consulted;
- Meeting and contacting;
- Negotiating and bargaining;
- Communicating;

- Co-ordinating;
- Co-operating;
- Synergising (making the total equal more than the sum of the parts, as when a team works so well together it seems they just cannot put a foot wrong, yet if they were working individually the result would not be as good).

Clearly, in this chapter we are concerned with the second group of skills. In any case, most people are adequately trained in the technical side of their work. Clearly, also, many kinds of problems can occur in each area, making an easy listing of problems a virtual impossibility.

Your success in your organisation will depend in large measure on how well you deal with the other people in it. You might find it useful to carry out a variation of the exercise you did earlier. Make a list of all the people you are responsible for. Now list the strengths and weaknesses of each one. You could do it in two columns, with a third one on the left for their names. Doing this may help you to identify ways of motivating your people better or of improving their abilities. We shall return to the topic of motivation later. You might also, incidentally, make a list of your own strengths and weaknesses. I wonder how many readers will then have the courage to show the list to their subordinates and ask if they agree with it. Those bold enough to do it might be in for some surprises, even shocks, but some interesting and potentially instructive ones nevertheless.

Everyone in an organisation has a role, a function, a part to play and everyone should be clear about what their role is. In most organisations of any size, roles are organised in a hierarchy and it is possible to draw an organisation chart to show people exactly where they fit in the total picture. If you do not have an organisation chart, you might find it a useful exercise to make one out. Start at the top and then work down the levels of authority, showing with solid lines who reports to whom. Show with dotted lines any other reporting procedures which exist. One thing to look out for is a situation in which someone reports to more than one person equally. This is undesirable. It is far better if people have only one superior to report to.

Look at the chart to see how many people report to each manager or supervisor. If this is more than about eight, it could be too many as the more people someone is responsible for the less time they have to devote to each one. The number of levels of authority in an organisation should be kept to a minimum because the more levels there are, the greater the risk of communication failures and the greater the possibility of people becoming alienated because they see themselves as being in a big, impersonal organisation. The authority that each person in the hierarchy has should be proportional to the responsibility they have. It certainly is not a good idea for someone to have authority without responsibility, but it is also undesirable to have people responsible for things they do not really have the authority to control, like making someone responsible for petty cash and not giving them a key to the safe.

People will be clearer as to their role in the organisation if their jobs are clearly defined. Each person should have more than the statutory minimum in terms of job description. A clear, unambiguous, detailed job specification enables people to know exactly where they stand. Written properly, a job specification will still allow for some flexibility for unforeseen or emergency situations to be covered. Only carelessly written specifications result in people refusing to do things because it is not their job. Besides, people usually only react like that if there are many other things wrong with the organisational climate. To ensure that this is as good as it can be made and to ensure that people's relationships with each other contribute to rather than hinder the success of the organisation, a spirit of teamwork has to be created and maintained. How your people react in a sudden crisis will give you a good idea of whether they are, and feel they are, a good team or not.

You can improve the team spirit of your people if everybody understands everybody else's job and what others' roles are in relation to their own. They will work together better if they understand and support the organisation's objectives. It will also help if you can encourage them to discuss problems that arise and give them the chance to have an input with major decisions. Even if something appears only to affect one member of a team, the others will feel they are part of the team if they are also consulted. Furthermore, the individual affected will feel better because of the reassurance that they have the backing of the team for what they are doing. They will feel less isolated.

Do what you can to make sure that where your staff work is as suitable as it can be. Obviously factors like safety, heating, light and noise need to be checked. If there is something wrong with any of these, it may have consequences far in excess of any cost of putting it right. One major decision may be whether to have open plan or separate offices. Often organisations opt for open plan on grounds of cost and then find that the people in the office spend more time creating barriers to give themselves some definable territory than working to achieve the organisation's objectives. You have to be sure that the workspace layout meets the needs of both the job and the people. If it does, it will usually be the most cost effective one in the long run anyway.

Another major problem area at the current time lies in getting people to respond to change in a positive way. It is a cliché to say that we live in an age of change, but true nonetheless. If you have to introduce changes, as you almost inevitably will, into your organisation or the part of it you are responsible for, there are certain principles and procedures you will need to bear in mind. For a start, people need time to adjust. You need to prepare people as far in advance as possible. There should be no surprises and no sudden shocks out of the blue. Generally speaking, the bigger the change, the more time and preparation people need in order to be able to cope with it. Keep them fully informed at all times and make sure they are genuinely consulted. Timing needs to be managed carefully, too. You should find that the more open you are about the changes needed, the more likely people are to understand the need for change and come to accept it sooner. If there have to be negotiations, make sure everybody has the fullest possible information and agrees with and supports the outcome. There will be little point in winning the argument in the short term if you are going to lose it in the long term.

In both times of change and times of stability, people like to have targets to achieve. In order to stimulate and motivate people, these targets should be set at an achievable level. All the targets of the various members of your team should stem from the overall targets for the group. There is no point in having people shooting off in different directions. This can happen, especially if you succumb to the greatest temptation when setting targets – opting for those which are easy to measure. These might not be the most useful ones. You will also need to monitor progress towards objectives.

Targets are easier to achieve when people are encouraged. Most of us like to do a job well and also be able to see where it fits into the plan as a whole. Most of us like to be told when we have done a good job. We like to feel that we have some control over our destiny and that those placed in authority over us are keeping us informed and up-to-date. If team members are not performing as they should, it may be necessary to criticise what they are doing. You should always remember, however, to criticise *behaviour* and not the individuals themselves. Most of the time it is not the people who are bad but what they have done. If you criticise the person, they will assume that your criticism applies to everything they do and this is a powerful de-motivator. You are thus creating more problems for yourself rather than solving one.

When people leave your organisation or the part of it that you are responsible for, do you ask yourself why? If you find it difficult to recruit the right people, do you ask yourself why? Ignoring questions like these is a quick way to get into trouble. It is a big temptation to put the blame on people when things go wrong, to dismiss them or let them leave and look for replacements outside. The grass is always greener there. But the new recruits may well be no better. You would do well to switch to improving the people you have rather than embark upon a potentially fruitless search elsewhere. Training is vital. It is necessary to ensure that the work is done properly and it also makes people feel more confident.

Training should be related to your overall objectives and should be carried out simultaneously with the development of the business as a whole. Training should not just help people to do their jobs better. It should make them generally more aware, more curious, more inventive and more concerned to see the organisation succeed. Training may be carried out in many ways. There are college courses, seminars run by independent consultants, books like this one, computer-based training and open learning (where an individual works his or her way through a package of learning materials at his or her own pace, location and time). It is important to be flexible and creative in selecting the method by which the training is done. Individuals learn best in different ways at different times and for different kinds of material. The principal techniques by which people learn are:

- Explanation
- Demonstration
- Experiment
- Trial and error
- Correction of errors by others
- Punishment
- Reward
- Imitation of models of good practice
- Practice and exercises
- Feedback on performance

- Observation
- Necessity
- Readiness to learn
- Motivation
- Experience
- Problem-solving
- Insight
- Chance
- Critical incidents (for example, suddenly becoming motivated to learn a foreign language by meeting an attractive young Swedish girl)
- Maturation (certain things are learned best at certain ages, for example, it is probably better to talk to people of 18 rather than 16 about their responsibilities in society because at 18 they do at least have a vote)
- Analogy
- Imagination
- Rote and repetition
- Questioning
- Discussion
- Introspection
- Deduction
- Drawing inferences
- Becoming aware of implications
- Critical analysis of performance

You should explore and experiment a little to find which of these methods works best for you and your people.

In the years to come, one thing is certain: those who do not train people in more than just job skills will find it even harder to recruit the right kind of staff and will find themselves falling further and further behind their competitors.

In many situations people respond quite willingly and spontaneously and do whatever is required of them. On other occasions, they may need to be led. You will need to be a good leader. Some people believe that leaders are born and not made, but there are things you can do to enhance your own skills in this area. You can be sure that you understand the role of the leader, for one thing.

A leader must be able to command the commitment and the co-operation of his or her team. He or she must be able to get the group into action. A leader must be able to make the best use of the various skills and abilities of the members of the team. He or she must be able to get the job done through a proper use of whichever are the relevant management skills that we looked at on pages 152–154. You must have a clear picture of your objectives, what tasks need to be done to achieve them and how they need to be done. You must make sure that team members know how they are going to reach their targets. They should also know what rewards and punishments will be used if the objectives are not met.

The leader must also be able to establish and maintain good relationships with and within the team. This means you must find time to listen to them and not just when they have a work-related problem. You should be reasonably friendly and approachable, while always being able to exert your authority when necessary. Treat the team members as equals on the same kind of basis. Be aware of the individual needs, aspirations and ambitions within the team and help them to achieve those which will benefit not just the organisation but the individual as well.

Some born leaders are very imposing and charismatic individuals, but you can move a long way towards enjoying the kind of success they enjoy by using the skills of observation, analysis and communication which some of the chapters in this book have sought to help you to develop. Good leadership involves being able to delegate work to team members. From your point of view, delegation is a desirable skill because it frees you from many routine and less important jobs. It leaves you able to do more of the planning, organising, motivating and controlling that a manager should be doing. It means decisions can be made more quickly, rather than having to wait until you have the time to make them, and decisions are made at the level where there is the greatest knowledge of all the circumstances.

Delegation is another method of staff development and training. You should look for opportunities to delegate when you have more work to do than you have available time in which to do it. You should delegate when you do not have enough time to do the top priority aspects of your work properly. You should never do a job yourself which could quite adequately be done by one of your subordinates. When you delegate, you should be very clear about exactly what the task is you are delegating. You should be clear as to who is to do the work, how they are to do it, when it is to be done by and how progress is to be monitored. You should be clear as to what powers of decision making you are delegating and under what circumstances they must come back to you before proceeding.

Delegation is a powerful way of motivating people, because with delegation they can see very clearly how and why they are more involved in the organisation's activities. There are other things you can do to develop your abilities in motivating others. You should have a clear understanding of what your team members' needs are for a sense of security, self-esteem and self-fulfilment. You should be aware of their expectations for the future. People can become very embittered and de-motivated if they see themselves being captains of industry and no one advises them that they will never make it and they have to find out for themselves through being stuck in the same job for many years.

The development of the team spirit itself is a strong motivator because when people are working together in the pursuit of common goals the members of the team will help one of their number who is experiencing difficulties of whatever kind at any time. Group pressures will also be brought to bear upon those who are perceived as not quite pulling their full weight. This is more likely to have a productive effect on such people than any stick that you might wield.

Evaluation

Write down the things that you can do in the foreseeable future to improve the way in which you manage people. You may take this to mean people in your team at work, people in any organisation in which you are the chair or secretary or occupy some other kind of managerial role, or even your immediate family. It might even be an enlightening exercise to do it for all three, but it is up to you. This is an area in which you will have to exercise your own judgment in deciding just how far whatever you have learned from this chapter can be put to practical use. After all, you are the only person who knows the people you have to deal with.

Ongoing

You will find that your skill in managing people will continue to improve if you carry out some of the following activities regularly:

- Periodically check the details of your own job, your objectives and the people you have to work through to achieve them to see if any improvements can be made.
- Have regular detailed talks with each member of your team about their work, objectives, problems, etc.
- Keep a record of the achievements of the members of your team, whether these are work-related or not.

- Carry out a survey amongst your team to see what training opportunities they would most welcome in the future.
- If you do not have one, establish a staff appraisal system for your team in which you review the performance of each member, with them, annually with a view to identifying ways of generating improved performance.

Completion checklist

At the end of this chapter you should be able to answer the following questions:

1. What is the most important resource any organisation has?
2. Into which two broad categories might we classify the skills of managing people?
3. What will make people clearer as to their role in an organisation?
4. When are targets easier to achieve?
5. How many of the ways in which people learn can you list?
6. How can you move towards enjoying the success that born leaders achieve?
7. What should you be clear about when you delegate work to others?

Conclusion

Of all the topics covered in this book, this is perhaps the one above all others where improvement can be maintained almost indefinitely. People are such complex beings that, no matter how well we think we know them, there is always more to learn. This learning can help us continuously to do better in our dealings with them, not only to improve the effectiveness of the organisation but also to increase everybody's chances of enjoying a richer, more rewarding life.

You should find it useful to review the points made in this chapter periodically, perhaps just before you review the performance of your team to see if it has achieved what it set out to do and to set its objectives for the period immediately ahead.

Review what you have learned from this chapter before you go to sleep tonight.

14

TIME MANAGEMENT

Time is a finite resource. It cannot be recycled like many other resources. It can only be used or allowed to pass by. No one who works in a modern organisation can afford to let the latter happen. Time is so valuable that it must be used effectively.

Here you will be introduced to techniques of recording activities in such a way that their implications in the use of time are made clear. There will be an examination of the use of time in specific aspects of organisational life and discussion of some of the principal problems and opportunities in using time more effectively.

There will be an emphasis throughout on using time management techniques to create new time which you will be able to use for either work or leisure related purposes as you wish.

Review

In this chapter, the Review is in two parts. First of all, complete the Activity Record on page 164, either for the past week (if you can remember what you did in sufficient detail) or for one week from tomorrow.

Make enough copies of the Activity Record to enable you to do this.

Do not read on until you have done this.

Secondly, complete the checklist on page 165 on the use of time.

Figure 14.1 Activity Record Date: ______________

Goals: 1 ____________________ 4 ____________________
2 ____________________ 5 ____________________
3 ____________________ 6 ____________________

Time	Activity	Priority	Action Taken
0830			
0900			
0930			
1000			
1030			
1100			
1130			
1200			
1230			
1300			
1330			
1400			
1430			
1500			
1530			
1600			
1630			
1700			
1730			
1800			
Evening			

Priorities
1 = Important & urgent 3 = Urgent, not important
2 = Important, not urgent 4 = Routine

Comments and Evaluation ....
....

Make a copy of this one for future use before you complete it.

Figure 14.2 The use of time: a checklist

Here is a list of the factors that many people working in organisations have identified as causing them to make inefficient use of their time. Tick the ones that you consider your own time wasters.

Unclear objectives	...
Inadequate information on which to act	...
Postponed decisions	...
Procrastination	...
Lack of feedback on whether you have done the right thing	...
Routine work	...
Too much reading	...
Interruptions	...
The telephone	...
No time planning	...
Meetings	...
Lack of competent personnel to work with	...
Lack of delegation	...
Lack of self-discipline	...
Visitors	...
Training new staff	...
Lack of priorities	...
Unavailability of people	...
Junk mail	...
Outside demands (i.e., any not related to your job)	...
Poor filing system	...
Fatigue	...
Questionnaires	...
Socialising	...
Lack of concentration	...
Coffee and tea breaks	...
Unintelligible communications	...
Lack of clerical staff	...
Red tape	...
Pet projects	...

contd. overleaf

Attempting too much at once ...
Span of control (having too many subordinates to supervise) ...
Usurped authority (having your decisions overridden) ...
Can't say no ...
Low morale ...
Mistakes ...
Overoptimism (thinking you can do more than is possible) ...
Employees with problems ...
Failure to listen (by yourself or by others) ...
Responding to the urgent rather than the important ...
Confused responsibilities ...
Failure to motivate staff ...
Lack of co-ordination ...
Waiting for decisions ...
Lack of monitoring and review procedures ...
Orientation towards problems rather than opportunities ...

Add to the list any other sources of time wasting that you feel apply to your job.

The Activity Record should help you to see how you are using your time at the moment. It may even reveal particular problems on certain days or at certain times of day. It may also reveal that, for instance, you are less likely to be interrupted at 3.30 pm than any other time of day. If 'windows' like this occur, it may be worth saving them for particularly important tasks.

The checklist on the use of time should help you to pin down which aspects of time use are your greatest problems. You should then keep an eye out for the places in this chapter where the solution is offered. Just in case you miss a solution or it is not specifically covered in what follows, there is a brief list at the end of the chapter of the main methods of dealing effectively with each aspect of time use mentioned in the checklist.

Do not read on until you have completed the Activity Record and checklist

Problems

In this chapter, most of the problems that are likely to be experienced in the use of time have already been identified in the use of time checklist. (You should, however, list any others which are a problem for you personally and which are not on the list.)

Objectives

The basic objectives you should have (though you should, of course, add some specific objectives of your own to the list) are:

- Recording the use of time in such a way that opportunities for using it more effectively are revealed;
- Identifying the key issues in time management;
- Using time more effectively in all everyday activities;
- Solving problems in the use of time;
- Identifying opportunities for the more effective use of time in organisations;
- Using the techniques of chronemics (which will be explained later) to create time which you can then use for whatever purposes you choose.

Methods

If you are to improve your management of time, you need an effective strategy. As with the other skills we have looked at, you need to develop a systematic approach. This is not going to be as difficult as you might suppose because you have already put into effect the first two elements of the strategy – assessing how you use your time at present and setting objectives for the use of time.

The next step is to examine all the activities you have to engage in over the next day, week, month or whatever period you think is most appropriate for you, and determine your priorities. These will be the tasks which will help you to achieve your objectives. Anything which does not do this is not a priority.

There are several ways of defining priorities. The two most common ones are to place tasks into (*1*) four categories or (*2*) three categories. In the first method, you should rate your tasks as:

- Important and urgent;
- Important, but not urgent;
- Urgent, but not important;
- Neither important nor urgent, i.e. routine.

In the second method, you classify tasks as A, B, or C level tasks, where A tasks are the most important ones. When you have finished, you look at the B tasks and re-classify them as A or C. Then you put the C tasks to one side and concentrate on completing the A tasks. It is for you to decide which method best meets your needs.

Once you have set your priorities, you need to produce a plan for the next day, week, month or whatever period of time you have selected. Most people will find that a general yearly plan, with a more detailed monthly plan and a most detailed weekly plan will enable them to manage their time most effectively. Your plan should tell you what you have to do.

You should list everything you want to do in the time period you have chosen. You are producing what is, in effect, a projected record. Estimate the time required for each task and set deadlines. If, as you begin to work through the plan, new items raise themselves, add them to the bottom of the list, unless there are compelling reasons for placing them higher. Cross off completed items. Ask yourself: What do I want to have accomplished by the end of the time period I have chosen? What activities will help me to achieve my objectives? This will help you to keep your attention clearly focused on them and not lose sight of them when under the pressures of the daily hurly-burly.

The plan should lead to the production of a schedule or diary for the advance time period you have selected. Most people find it best to work on a weekly plan, which is completed in 20–30 minutes on a Friday for the week ahead. This is supplemented by a daily plan, completed in 15–20 minutes at the end of each day, for the following day. You may need to vary this to suit your particular circumstances. For instance, in addition to writing books, I present seminars in the various subjects covered in these books. I need, therefore, to work on a much longer time scale than most people. I plan for a period of time months ahead to ensure that (as happened one week before I began practising time management) I am not in Glasgow on Monday, Ipswich on Tuesday and Wednesday and Cardiff on Thursday and Friday. As I live in Sunderland on the North East coast of England, this was not a well-planned week. As most seminars are planned at least two or three months ahead and sometimes as much as a year or more in advance, it is not usually critical to the client whether it is held in one week or the next. This pattern also means that a weekly plan and a daily plan are of little use to me, since I know where I will be and what I shall be doing and people rarely have to cancel seminars. If they do, I usually get at least two weeks' notice. My days and weeks are planned for me, if you like. I need to control the pattern of location and duration of seminars much further ahead.

When it comes to putting your plan and the schedule into action, one or two points are worth bearing in mind, especially if you have to plan daily or weekly. It helps if you can leave 25 per cent of each day unplanned in order to cope with the unexpected. This is what many time management experts recommend. If you cannot achieve this, see just how much flexibility you can build in. Your activity record should help you at this point.

Do the most important things first. This should ensure that you begin the day by concentrating on the items that really matter. When unscheduled items, like interruptions, occur, stop for a moment. Ask yourself: Is this interruption more important than what I was doing? If it isn't, try to find a tactful way of putting the interrupter off until a more convenient moment later in the day.

Plan for waiting time. There are always occasions on which you cannot make progress because a telephone number is engaged or someone else's meeting overruns and delays the start of yours. Have tasks ready for times like these, so that you are not left looking out of the window tapping your fingers irritatedly on the desk.

Remember to keep an activity record. It is not enough only to do one at the beginning of a course of training such as this. It should be a regular task. At the very least, it should be something you do several times a year to check that you are not slipping back into bad habits.

For those who doubt the wisdom of spending so much time planning, believing that it is better to concentrate on doing things rather than getting ready to do them, it is worth remembering that at least half of planned activities work out. In other words, there is a better than 50 per cent chance that an activity will take place as planned.

'Procrastination (putting things off) is the thief of time' is an old quote, but a true one. You need to eliminate the habit of procrastinating, for it is just that – a habit. And habits can be broken.

Put unpleasant activities early in the day. That way, you can deal with them when you are at your freshest. It also means that the rest of the day will be more pleasant and enjoyable.

Break big, difficult tasks into smaller ones. The Chinese have a saying that 'A journey of a thousand miles begins with a single step.' Breaking a task up is rather like taking this single step. It makes it easier to start and it is surprising how quickly the steps mount up until you find you have covered quite a distance.

When you have completed a task, give yourself some kind of reward. This could be anything from a sweet or a cup of coffee to something much more substantial, depending on the size of the task. Rewards help to provide motivation on those occasions when you just do not feel like doing anything.

Study how other people use their time to good effect. You might, for instance, note the techniques that other people use on you to close meetings and discussions or the techniques they use to avoid being stopped from proceeding by interruptions. The average manager is interrupted every eight or nine minutes. You should ask yourself: 'How will this interruption help me to reach my objective? Do I have to be interrupted now?' If you cannot avoid an interruption, make sure that you get back on course as quickly as possible. Plan and allow for interruptions. Then if they happen, you can deal with them. If they do not, you can do something else that you have to do.

Periodically, review your use of time and assess the degree of your success. If things went wrong, ask yourself why. If you are a manager, you might consider asking your staff how you could manage your time better. You might even ask them how you could help them to use their time more effectively. The responses might be quite illuminating.

Above all, give yourself the motto: **'DO IT NOW'**.

In addition to these methods, there are twelve techniques drawn from chronemics, which is the name given to the study of the use of time, which may be helpful. The techniques can be described briefly like this:

1 **Speed an activity up** slightly until you are doing things as quickly as you can and still achieve the quality of performance you require.
2 **Set deadlines** by which tasks or even parts of tasks have to be completed. Try to allow for some 'slack' in case things do not proceed as smoothly as planned.
3 **Use flexible performance strategies**, that is to say, systematic approaches to tasks. A typical strategy might take this form:

Select an activity. Time it and assess the quality of performance. Set objectives to be achieved. Each time you undertake the task, use whichever of the twelve techniques outlined here seem most appropriate. After about two weeks, assess how much progress you have made. If necessary, you can repeat the process until you have exhausted the potential for improvement.

4 **Use anticipatory scanning techniques**: Before you start a task, look ahead to see what kinds of things are going to be involved and plan accordingly. This technique is often practised by people in public contact occupations where they may have a queue of people to deal with. The better operators will look down the line periodically so that they can quickly adapt their approach to a different kind of person from the one they are currently dealing with.
5 **Be selective in your perception of cues.** This means that you give your closest attention to the key features in a situation. There are many occasions on which it is impossible to deal with everything, so you deal with the most important ones. It is rather like dealing with 'A' category tasks, as explained earlier, and leaving 'C' category tasks until the end.
6 **Keep records of the way you do things.** This will provide you with valuable feedback on your performance. You have to have reliable information about what you have been doing if you are to make sensible decisions about changing behaviour.
7 **Set aside a little time** – life's natural breaks like coffee breaks, lunch breaks, overnight breaks will help to let things mull over in your mind. These 'incubation periods' can be very useful in helping you to stand back from what you have been doing and look at it more objectively. They help you to separate the wood from the trees.
8 **Always allow for imaginative and intuitive responses** because sometimes you 'just know' the right thing to do without having to think about it or plan ahead.
9 **Keep your mind open** for the occurrence of critical incidents and learning periods. Critical incidents are those which give you a sudden and unexpected insight into the nature of a problem or its solution. Learning periods are those times when you are most receptive to new information, ideas or experiences.

10 **Try to time things just right** and try to move smoothly and easily from one activity to another. Try to synchronise the various parts of an activity and get them to dovertail neatly with each other.
11 **Have a 'reserve bank' of activities ready** for those times when you cannot proceed with a task through no fault of your own; for example, when someone else has to do something before you can make further progress.
12 **Periodically analyse your performance** critically. Study your records and try to see how and where further improvement is necessary and how you might achieve it.

As you can see, there are many techniques that you can use to bring about improvements in your use of time. However, of all the aspects of the use of time that can affect the way in which it is managed, five stand out as being of particular importance. If you can improve your use of time in these key respects, you will find that you use your time generally more efficiently and effectively.

First, you must identify waste in the use of time. Use the checklist provided at the beginning of this chapter to find out where you recognise you are not using your time to the best effect. Identify and add any other activities that waste time which are not listed. In doing this, consider carefully what you mean by a time wasting activity, for they are not the same for everyone. One person may, for instance, regard meetings as being a source of wasted time, but another may reasonably regard them as being an essential part of his or her work.

Secondly, set clear objectives and define priorities. In time management, as in any other activity, it helps if you can specify your objectives. Remember to distinguish carefully between an aim and an objective. An aim tells you the direction in which you intend to travel. An objective tells you how far in that direction you intend to go at the present time. Activities should, as we have seen, be ranked in order of priority.

Thirdly, use techniques of time scheduling. The basic technique of scheduling is to use a diary in a form most suited to your tasks. Some people will need only a brief daily guide, others will need an appointments diary where the day is split into half-hour slots. Review your schedule periodically to make sure you are not sliding back into older, less organised habits and to evaluate whether or not your allocation of priorities is appropriate. Keep a close watch on how well you achieve your objectives for the use of time.

Next, delegate. Check through your activities to identify those which can be delegated to others. Remember that delegating implies supervising and monitoring. Simply to hand over something to someone else to do without making sure that it has been done is abdication. It is possible that you may find that there are degrees in the extent to which activities can be delegated. Some can be delegated wholly, others only in part, others for part of the time, and so on. Keep in mind, if you are a manager, that delegation, effectively used, is a powerful instrument for staff development. After all, people cannot be expected to acquire the ability to act responsibly and with initiative unless they are given the scope to do so. See Chapter 13 for more on delegation.

Finally, examine routines and the use of time they involve. One of the problems with routines is that people may continue an activity after it has outlived its usefulness simply because: 'We have always done it this way.' Review your routines regularly and make sure they fulfil a purpose. Examine the steps that make up a routine to see if any can be eliminated.

Evaluation

In this chapter, the Evaluation is in two parts. It follows the same basic pattern as the Review stage you completed at the beginning of the chapter so that you can make comparisons and see how far you have progressed. First of all, complete the Activity Record on page 164 either for the past week (if you can remember what you did in sufficient detail) or for one week from tomorrow. Make enough copies of the Activity Record to enable you to do this.

Do not read on until you have done this.

Secondly, complete the checklist on the use of time on page 165.

Do not read on until you have done this.

What differences do you note between your responses now and your responses at the beginning of the chapter? Where have you made your greatest improvements? Where have you failed to make much progress at all? Do you have any ideas about why this should be? Is there anything you can do to remedy the situation? Would it help to work through the relevant parts of this chapter again? Principally, you should look at your achievements and perhaps consider that not everyone can improve in every respect on everything. You should now build upon your areas of success.

Ongoing

There is an old saying about the way organisations work which, roughly paraphrased, runs: 'It is all very well having objectives and priorities, backed up by systematic approaches, but when you are up to your ears in crocodiles it is difficult to remind yourself that your original objective was to clear the swamp.' Some of the problems in putting time management to work are considered in this section, but there is also a positive side and the opportunities offered by the techniques we have looked at are considered as well.

One problem, for instance, can be 'firefighting'. If you find yourself diverted from your time schedule to deal with too many urgent crises, you have to find some time in which you can reflect on what is going wrong. You may have to use a little of your own free time to do this. If it produces one or two practical solutions, it will have been time well spent. Try to identify those crises which, with a little forethought (even though you are now using hindsight) could have been avoided. Be ready for them the next time they arise.

Allow some time in your time scheduling for the unexpected, even if it does mean that occasionally you do have to say to someone politely but firmly, 'No, I can't do that at the moment because this has to be done.' If you can then tell them when you do expect to be able to say 'Yes, I can do that now', that may do the trick. You should find that planning a little further ahead than you have been accustomed to might also help.

If you have a superior to report to (and most people have), try to present matters requiring his or her attention in good time. Know the full range of his or her responsibilities and activities in the organisation. Try to help in organising his or her time where you tactfully can. Try to see him or her early in the day if you require 'marching orders'. If you control your boss's calls, visitors and mail, screen them so that he or she can concentrate on those which really matter. Above all, try to establish a close, trusting and thoroughly professional working relationship.

In continuing to develop your own time management techniques, as in all other forms of self-training, follow the classic formula embodied in the questions:

- Where am I now (present level of performance)?
- Where do I want to go (setting objectives and priorities)?
- How will I get there (choosing appropriate training methods)?
- How will I know I've arrived (new level of performance)?
- Where do I go next (continuation and follow-up work)?

Periodically, review your activity records and diary, looking for conspicuous successess and failures. Once your time is better organised, allow some 'thinking time' in your day to check that all the requirements of effective time management are being met. Work through the checklist on the use of time occasionally and concentrate your attention on stubborn areas that seem to resist improvement.

Finally, decide on the most useful period for you for forward planning and complete the Action Plan overleaf. In future, do this at the beginning of each forward planning period.

Completion checklist

At the end of this chapter you should be able to answer the following questions:

1. What should the Activity Record help you to see?
2. Which two methods of defining priorities are described?
3. How much of your day should you try to leave unplanned?
4. Which tasks should you tackle first each day?
5. What other kinds of tasks should you put early in the day?
6. What is the motto you should give yourself?
7. How many of the techniques of chronemics can you list?
8. What is the basic technique of time scheduling?
9. What is one of the problems with routines?
10. What is 'firefighting'?
11. For what should you allow some time in your time scheduling?

Conclusion

In addition to revising your recollection of the points made in this chapter about time management, you will find it useful to look back over previous chapters and try to identify time management aspects of the other skills we have tried to improve in this book. Since all skills inevitably involve the use of some time in their performance, you should find that there are many more insights to be gained into how you can use (indeed, how you are using) your time more effectively.

Review what you have learned from this chapter before you go to sleep tonight.

ACTION PLAN

Task	*Priority*	*Deadline*	*Results to be achieved*	*Action to be taken*

15

HOW TO USE S.T.E.P.S. TO IMPROVE ANY SKILL

You will probably have deduced by now that the approach taken to improve each of the skills in this book could be used to develop any skill. You will have noticed that the pattern of each chapter is the same:

1 Some introductory text
2 Review
3 Problems
4 Objectives
5 Methods
6 Evaluation
7 Ongoing
8 Completion checklist
9 Conclusion

Not all of these elements are always necessary for successful self-instruction, as we shall see below. Problems could be considered as part of the Review. They have been treated separately here for the sake of emphasising their existence and because it is assumed that many people reading this book may not have undergone any form of training for several years, therefore they may experience more problems than people who are used to being involved in training programmes of various kinds. Similarly, the introductory text and the conclusion could be regarded as not actually being part of the skills improvement.

The individual parts of the approach, however, do not make much sense on their own. They need to be fitted into a theoretical and a practical framework. Once that is done, you should be able to devise and run self-improvement programmes for any skill. It is the purpose of this chapter to provide you with just such a framework.

Since all the skills dealt with in this book are either wholly or partly communication skills, I have based the approach to their improvement on what I have called '*edetics*'. This is simply a convenient acronym to encapsulate the thesis that '**Everyone Develops Effectiveness Through Improving Communication Skills**'. The word should not be confused with 'eidetic', which is a psychological term commonly used in the phrase 'eidetic imagery' – technical language for a photographic memory. In a corporate context, I have often referred to edetics as '*mandetics*', which stands for '**Management Develops Effectiveness Through Improving Communication Skills**'. Those who are studying this book as part of a business or industrial or professional self-training (or even group training) programme may prefer to use the term mandetics as a label for the approach.

It is my view that before you can improve other skills, you must first improve communication skills. Once this has been done to whatever level of competence an individual is capable of, the same methods can be used to improve any other skill you choose. This is why I regard the skills covered in this book as the essential personal skills.

Theoretically, edetics rests on certain basic assumptions about the nature of the communication process and about how one develops as a person. It assumes the inevitability of communication. We cannot *not* communicate, if you like. Social life would be impossible without the ability to communicate. It assumes, therefore, that the major factor in an individual's growth and development as a person is his or her ability to increase skill in communicating with others. These propositions are 'taken for granted', that is, no proof is offered to support them. This is because it seems impossible to verify or disprove them empirically. Such a task would demand a control over the many variables involved which would be unattainable in practice. These propositions do, however, seem to be justified within a 'common sense' definition of the situation. You must, in the final analysis, decide for yourself whether or not you can accept them as being true in the light of your own knowledge and experience of people and of the world around you.

Edetics further assumes that for communication to take place successfully, in most contexts, the exercise of skill is required and that communication skills are always capable of improvement. It assumes that these skills can be trained to a higher level of performance and that the most effective way of achieving this is by pursuing the aims, and using the methods, described below.

Aims

The primary aims of edetics may be summarised in the following acronym: TALENT. To be an effective communicator, an individual needs to be:

Thinking
Articulate
Literate
Empathic
Numerate
Tolerant

These terms require a little clarification of their meanings as they are used in the context of this book.

'Thinking' is taken to include 'thoughtful' as well as to indicate that an individual is skilled in both convergent and divergent thinking. 'Thoughtfulness' is seen as being closer to critical thinking than to caring for, or having regard to, other people (though, of course, that too is a highly laudable aim). It is assumed that a thinking person needs to have a thoughtful and critical approach to his or her own knowledge and experience and, particularly, to skill in communicating.

'Articulate' may be taken to be more or less synonymous with what has come to be called 'oracy', or the ability to speak fluently when communicating with others. It implies that an effective speaker is able to plan and organise what he or she has to say, especially in encounters which have a higher degree of formal structure than ordinary social or casual conversation. An 'articulate' person should, for instance, be able to request or give information, advice, opinions, and so on, in the kind of ordered and logical manner that promotes ease of understanding and which is generally recognised as showing skill in expression.

'Literate' as it is used here should not be confused with 'literary' but should be allied with the concept of 'literacy' or the ability to read and comprehend a wide range of materials written in various ways, some of which may have a quite high level of difficulty. In other words, it means that an individual can perform successfully the sophisticated reading tasks required of a competent participant in our increasingly complex society. It also means that an individual has a degree of skill in written expression that is of a fairly high order.

'Empathic' can be thought of as encompassing the range of abilities that are demanded when you, as a non-participant, try to view a situation as if you were, and more particularly, to view it from the standpoint of one identified participant. The more successfully a person can assume the role of the other in this way, the more empathic he or she may be thought to be.

'Numerate' means having the requisite degree of skill in handling numbers, calculations and methods of quantifying demanded of a fully integrated member of our society. In this book, since numeracy is not normally considered to be one of the communication skills, this aspect of effectiveness in communication is only considered in relation to, and as made necessary by, work designed to improve the use of the skills discussed (for example, calculating the Fog Index in the chapter on writing). This is not to devalue numeracy, but simply to leave the exploration of its full impact as an aspect of edetics to others more skilled – that is, to those who are more 'numerate'.

'Tolerant' is seen to be equivalent to a willingness to consider other points of view and, more than this, to tolerate their continued and justified existence. It is not meant to imply intellectual 'softness' or a willingness to turn a blind eye. The pursuit of truth is an honourable occupation, but a tolerant person recognises that there are many pathways to it and a difference in standpoint need not mean that the truth is hidden from view. Being 'tolerant' is, then, seen as being an indispensable element in a liberal education.

Liberal education is the ultimate aim of edetics. It is assumed that, if an individual is thinking, articulate, literate, empathic, numerate and tolerant, he or she is at least on the way to being capable of being regarded as liberally educated. Defining liberal education in this way, in terms of skills and abilities, makes it immediately less elitist and more democratic. Everyone in our society has the opportunity to develop these skills and abilities. Edetics training can provide the means whereby this opportunity can be realised. For the training to be fully effective, however, it has to be seen in an appropriate context. In our complex industrial society, and even in the emergent industrial societies of the Third World, people live in organisations. For our purposes here, even the family can be regarded as an organisation and certainly the work carried out by the bulk of the population is done within and for organisations. A universal feature of organisations is management. Even housepersons are managers (and there are many who would object to the 'even'). They fulfil all the requirements of management that have been laid down over time by various management writers.

In any organisation, a manager exercises many skills, as we saw in Chapter 13. For convenience (and for those who have not yet read Chapter 13 but perhaps out of curiosity have come straight to this chapter), these can be grouped into *intellectual* skills and *social* skills. Intellectual skills include planning, controlling, evaluating, forecasting, analysing, problem-solving, deciding, monitoring, diagnosing, investigating and initiating. Social skills include directing, supervising, co-ordinating, organising, leading, selling, motivating, encouraging, negotiating, consulting, competing, co-operating and communicating. This last is the core skill of management. If he or she is to do the job at all, a manager must be able to communicate effectively with others, therefore he or she needs to be *communication-centred* to be a good manager.

Communication-centred management promotes both personal and organisational development. It promotes personal growth and development because a person who communicates well becomes more effective in social interaction with others. Since we are social animals, it follows that through improving and developing our relationships with others we experience real personal growth. Communication-centred management also promotes organisational development because, if an individual improves and becomes a more effective member of an organisation, this makes the organisation as a whole more effective. The effect is cumulative and synergic (that is, the sum effect is greater than mere addition of the individual improvements would lead us to expect).

The concept of communication-centred management, like TALENT, is of fundamental importance in an edetics approach. If TALENT represents the primary aims of edetics, communication-centred management represents the prerequisite basis for achieving these aims, especially in an organisational context. The approach, however, is valid for both personal and organisational development, because of the links between the two described above.

Methods

In order to realise the aims discussed in the previous section, we need a systematic and planned strategy, a specific methodological framework, and effective techniques and skills to use and be developed within that framework. It is in offering these that edetics makes its new and unique contribution to training in essential personal skills. The approach has the mnemonic title PRO or PAPA-ROMEO-OSCAR (for a diagrammatic summary of this, see Figure 15.1 on page 185, based on letters in the phonetic alphabet).

The systematic general strategy ROMEO contains five stages, similar to those we have already seen at the beginning of this chapter:

Review
Objectives (general)
Methods
Evaluation
Ongoing

In following this strategy to improve the use of personal skills, the first step is to review the present level of performance. This involves a performance analysis (PA), using appropriate methods of testing and measurement so that a clear picture can be obtained of how well an individual uses a skill or skills at present, or how well these skills are used within an organisation, or how suited an organisation's communication systems are to its needs. This step can, however, be applied whatever the training problems to be overcome, situation to be studied, or aspect of individual or organisational life to be analysed and changed. It is essential to be able to answer the questions: 'Where are we now? Where have we come from? How did we get here?' before taking the next step.

Once the present picture is clear, we can then move on to the determination and definition of general objectives to be achieved. In other words, we attempt to answer the question: '*Where* do we want to go?' The clearer our destination becomes the better. In order to do this, objectives should be stated as results to be achieved rather than as intentions. The objectives given for the various skills in earlier chapters of this book exemplify the approach necessary. At this stage, all that is required is a statement of the *general* objectives to be achieved. More specific objectives and targets can be set during the next stage.

Armed with the information acquired so far and with a clear idea of what we want to do, we can now decide upon the methods we will use to reach our objectives. We can seek to answer the question: '*How* do we get there?' At this point, the methodological framework OSCAR, which is discussed below, comes into play and the methods used in improving skills are selected in the light of everything that is known about all the relevant factors. We should now be able to do whatever is necessary to enable the objectives to be reached.

Once training has been given, it is necessary to carry out a further PA or evaluation of the training. We have to be able to answer the question: 'Have we arrived?' This evaluation will usually take the form of tests and measurements that are sufficiently similar to the methods used at the Review stage to enable valid comparisons to be made. In this way, it becomes possible to attempt some quantification of how far objectives have been achieved. At this point a reasonable level of numeracy may be necessary for successful performance. The results will enable intelligent decisions to be made at the next stage and will also make it easier to convince others of the value and effectiveness of the training.

The final step is to decide the ongoing procedures to be followed. These may take the form of repetitions of the training process with more advanced materials to enable higher levels of performance to be achieved, or they may provide for continued monitoring to ensure that standards already achieved do not deteriorate, or they may take the form of periodic analytic reviews.

Within this general strategy, the specific methodological framework OSCAR has the following stages:

Objectives (specific)
Skills
Contexts
Attitudes
Resources

When methods are selected and used, the first step is to determine and define specific objectives and targets to be met. This involves a close definition of needs and desires to be satisfied. To do this, it is useful to have a clear definition (perhaps in most cases already clear from the general objectives) of aims and purposes relevant to this satisfaction of needs and desires. Overall, it should be possible to arrive at a precise definition of the objectives and targets to be achieved in satisfying these needs, desires, aims and purposes. It is also useful at this stage to make some assessment of one's expectations from the training. Whilst general objectives are bound to apply to a wide range of individuals, specific objectives and expectations will only apply fully to the relevant individual. It is important to remember that specific objectives should be phrased in similar terms to those already advocated for general objectives, that is, as results to be achieved.

Once specific objectives have been set, it becomes easier to select the appropriate skills needed in developing the skills being trained. For instance, in developing reading skills, one has to decide whether to place the emphasis on skimming skills or study skills or skill in avoiding regression, and so on, according to the precise needs of the individual. It is important to describe and specify the contexts in which personal skills are to be used. For instance, it would be quite inappropriate to use exactly the same kind of writing skills when writing a note for the milkman or a chatty letter to a friend that you would use in writing to the Inland Revenue objecting to an assessment they have made.

The next step is to identify and clarify the attitudes that individuals may bring to the use of personal skills and which may affect what takes place. Attempts should be made to identify negative attitudes such as prejudices, beliefs, emotions and feelings which may influence and perhaps even prevent the exercise of a personal skill effectively. It is also necessary to identify positive attitudes such as motivation, confidence, willingness to make an effort and persistence which will promote effectiveness.

Finally, the resources necessary for the training have to be compared with those which are already available to see if there is any significant deficiency in the latter which might prevent the objectives being achieved. There would not be much point in seeking to improve reading skills, say, if there were no materials available to read, nor much point in trying to improve writing skills if one did not have access to pen or pencil and paper.

This PAPA-ROMEO-OSCAR (or PRO) approach, then, is what we need if we are to improve any of our personal skills. It is the approach which has been used in this book and it is the one which you can now apply to improve performance in using any other skills which you wish to develop.

Figure 15.1 The PRO approach

PAPA-ROMEO-OSCAR

A Diagrammatic Representation

Performance Analysis ———	Review	
	Objectives (general)	
	Methods ———	Objectives (specific)
		Skills
		Contexts
		Attitudes
		Resources
Performance Analysis ———	Evaluation	
	Review	

ANSWERS TO QUESTIONS

Answers to questions in the Completion Checklist at the end of each of the skills improvement chapters, can be found in the text of the relevant chapter. To include all the answers here would mean repeating large parts of the instructional text.

Chapter 3

Evaluation

1 False analogy
2 Cause and effect
3 Jumping to conclusions
4 Over-generalising/statements not necessarily connected
5 Pan calling kettle black
6 Over-generalising
7 Acknowledged expert
8 Company kept (often called 'guilt by association')
9 Over-generalising/self-evident truth

Chapter 4

Evaluation

1 *b*; 2 *d*; 3 *d*; 4 *d*; 5 *a*; 6 *a*; 7 *c*; 8 *c*; 9 *c*; 10 *a*.

Chapter 6

Evaluation

1 *b*; 2 *c*; 3 *b*; 4 *a*; 5 *c*; 6 *b*.

Chapter 7

Reading Speed Conversion Table

Minutes	*Seconds*	1014 *words*	995 *words*
1	30	676	663
1	35	640	628
1	40	608	597
1	45	579	567
1	50	553	543
1	55	529	519
2	00	507	498
2	05	487	478
2	10	468	459
2	15	451	442
2	20	435	426
2	25	420	412
2	30	406	398
2	35	393	385
2	40	380	373
2	45	369	362
2	50	356	351
2	55	348	341
3	00	338	332
3	05	329	323
3	10	320	314
3	15	312	306
3	20	304	299
3	25	297	291
3	30	290	284
3	35	283	278
3	40	277	271
3	45	270	265
3	50	265	260

3	55	259	254
4	00	254	249
4	10	243	239
4	20	234	230
4	30	225	221
4	40	217	213
4	50	210	206
5	00	203	199
5	15	193	190
5	30	184	181
5	45	176	173
6	00	169	166
6	15	162	159
6	30	156	153
6	45	150	147
7	00	145	142
7	30	135	133
8	00	127	124
9	00	113	111
10	00	101	100

How To Be A Judge – Comprehension Test

1 *a*; 2 *b*; 3 *c*; 4 *b*; 5 *c*; 6 *a*; 7 *c*; 8 *a*; 9 *d*; 10 *d*.

How To Make Learning Fun – Comprehension Test

1 *c*; 2 *b*; 3 *a*; 4 *d*; 5 *d*; 6 *b*; 7 *c*; 8 *d*; 9 *c*; 10 *c*.

Chapter 8

Evaluation

1 *d*; 2 *a*; 3 *b*; 4 *c*; 5 *a*; 6 *b*; 7 *c*; 8 *d*; 9 *a*; 10 *b*.

Chapter 9

Evaluation

A report is an ordered statement which uses headings and subheadings. It gives the facts about a situation or problem. It may also outline the case for and/or against a proposal or discuss the likely or actual effects of a decision or course of action. It may even describe and assess the results of work or research or simply record a sequence of events. A report may offer judgment of facts. It may draw conclusions and/or recommend action. There may also be other evidence and visual material, usually in appendices. Normally, the report will be prefaced by a brief summary.

This version has a Fog Index of 11.4 – a big improvement on 26.6. Most Fog Index calculators regard a figure within the range 10–12 as 'Safe'. Below this is 'Easy' and above is 'Difficult'. My own view is that if you know your readers are fairly well versed in your subject you can take the figure up to about 16. If the figure is below 8, you have either miscalculated or written *Janet and John* or *Thomas the Tank Engine*. But then you might make a lot of money doing that!

FURTHER READING

* = Titles which are particularly recommended.

Chapter 3

Buzan, T., *How To Make The Most Of Your Mind*, Colt Books, 1977

* Chase, S., *Guide To Straight Thinking*, Harper & Row, 1956

Stebbing, L.S., *Thinking To Some Purpose*, Penguin, 1963

Thouless, R., *Straight And Crooked Thinking*, Pan Books, 1963

Chapter 4

Cropley, A.J., *Creativity*, Longman, 1967

De Bono, E., *Lateral Thinking: A Textbook of Creativity*, Ward Lock Educational, 1970

Hanks, K. and Parry, J.A., *Wake Up Your Creative Genius*, Kaufmann, 1983

* Koberg, D. and Bagnall, J., *The Universal Traveler: a soft systems guide to creativity, problem-solving and the process of reaching goals*, Kaufmann, 1981

Chapter 5

* Higbee, K.L., *Your Memory: How It Works And How To Improve It*, Piatkus, 1989

Hunter, I.M.L., *Memory*, Penguin, 1964

Lorayne, H. and Lucas, J., *The Memory Book*, Star, 1976

Chapter 6

* Maddox, H., *How To Study*, Pan Books, 1963

Chapter 7

De Leeuw, M. and E., *Read Better, Read Faster*, Penguin, 1965

* Wainwright, G.R., *Rapid Reading Made Simple*, Heinemann, 1972

Wainwright, G.R., *Towards Efficiency in Reading*, Cambridge University Press, 1968

Webster, G., *Read Well And Remember*, Pan Books, 1965

Chapter 8

Hirsh, R.O., *Listening: Processing Information Aurally*, Gorsuch-Scarisbrick, 1990

Johnson, I.M., *Developing The Listening Skills*, Educational Activities, 1989

Kinlaw, D.C., *Listening and Communicating Skills*, University Associates, 1990

Chapter 9

Baugh, L.S., Fryar, M. and Thomas, D., *Handbook for Business Writing*, NTC Business Books, 1986

Turk, C. and Kirkman, J., *Effective Writing*, Spon, 1982

* Wainwright, G.R., *Report Writing*, Management Update, 1984

Chapter 10

Gelb, M., *Present Yourself*, Aurum Press, 1988

Janner, G., *Complete Speechmaker*, Business Books, 1981

* Leeds, D., *Powerspeak*, Piatkus, 1989

Chapter 11

Lewis, D., *The Secret Language Of Success*, Bantam Press, 1989
Lyle, J., *Body Language*, Octopus, 1990
Pease, A., *Body Language*, Sheldon Press, 1981
* Wainwright, G.R., *Body Language*, Hodder & Stoughton, 1985

Chapter 12

Citrine, W., *ABC Of Chairmanship*, NCLC, 1947
Taylor H.M. and Mears, A.G., *The Right Way To Conduct Meetings, Conferences And Discussions*, Elliot, 1983
* Wainwright, G.R., *Meetings & Committee Procedure*, Hodder & Stoughton, 1987

Chapter 13

Armstrong, M., *How To Be A Better Manager*, Kogan Page, 1983
Johnson, R., *How To Manage People*, Business Books, 1984
* Sidney, E., Brown, M. and Argyle, M., *Skills With People*, Hutchinson, 1973

Chapter 14

Godefroy, C.H. and Clark, J., *The Complete Time Management System*, Piatkus, 1989
Lakein, A., *How To Get Control Of Your Time And Your Life*, Signet, 1973
* Mackenzie, R.A., *The Time Trap*, McGraw-Hill, 1972

INDEX